Kitchen Design

for the 21st Century

Kitchen
Design
for the 21st Century

Nancy Elizabeth Hill
John Driemen

Sterling Publishing Co., Inc.
New York

Acknowledgments

Nancy Hill and I would like to thank all the homeowners who graciously allowed us into their homes and let us disrupt their lives so that we could get the photographs that appear in this book. Without their generosity and cooperation this book could not have been produced, and we want to add a special thanks to the kitchen designers, builders, and decorators who took the time to talk with us about what they did for these homeowners. We also want to thank North Star Kitchens in Minneapolis, Abruzzo Kitchens in Chicago, and Kitchens by Deane in Stamford, Connecticut for opening up their showrooms to our camera, incurring what I'm sure was a certain inconvenience.

John Driemen would like to thank the staff at the Kroch Library at Cornell University in Ithaca, New York who allowed me to look through Rose Steidl's papers and publications and who granted us permission to publish some of the historical kitchen photographs in their collection. They went out of their way to treat me, a kitchen writer, like a visiting scholar.

Nancy would especially like to thank William and Montgomery. You guys are the best! Florence Hill for your inspiration, patience, and loving care of us all. To Gloria and Aldo, a heartfelt *mille grazie*. Also thanks to Stephen, Robert, Charmin and Doug Hill, and Thomas.

Rick, thanks for being there for the weather, witchiness and all else—still.

Thanks also to Mark and Cathy at Connecticut Photographics, the best damn lab and people out there. To Charles G. and Jan D. for all that soccer support. Thanks to Ben Horn, Karen P., Jackie K., Evelyn, Joe B., Dawn T., Mark F., Chuck Wow, Laurel C., and Elaine S.

Thank you to Cathy at Design within Reach, and Maureen O. Thanks to Chris Madden and Carolyn Schultz—you girls rock. To Kyle Riccoboni—stylist extraordinaire, and to Curt G., for sharing your friends and your great space at Carmel.

Both of us want to thank Paula Schlosser and Karen Nelson at Sterling Publishing Co., Inc. for their design insights, and we especially want to express our thanks and gratitude to Julie Trelstad, our editor at Sterling for her constant support of this project and her encouragement from start to finish.

In memory of Bob Sweet and his incredible sense of design, humor and joie de vivre and to all those Helen Mooneys out there who love to cook.

Copyright © 2006 by Nancy Elizabeth Hill and John Driemen

Published by Sterling Publishing Co., Inc. New York, New York

Designed and produced by Aquarians Custom Publishing

Printed in China

Library of Congress
Cataloging-in-Publication Data is available

Sterling ISBN-13: 978-1-4027-3224-9
ISBN-10: 1-4027-3224-4

10 9 8 7 6 5 4 3 2 1
First Edition

Introduction

Kitchen design has changed. The ideas behind kitchen design today are very different from those of just ten years ago. So different that we call this book *Kitchen Design for the 21st Century* to set it apart from the ideas of the 1990s. What these 21st century kitchens do and how they do it will determine kitchen design trends for the foreseeable future. Flexibility and adaptability will be the underlying themes that drive homeowners and the designers they hire.

The 21st century kitchen is a work center kitchen. If you aren't familiar with work center kitchens it's probably because you've grown up believing the only way to lay out an efficient kitchen is by following the rules of the kitchen work triangle. This just isn't so, especially with bigger kitchens. Some of the ideas in this book are brand new to this century, if not brand new to you. Some aren't, because they are not new; they were developed almost sixty years ago, but only infrequently applied to kitchen design until recently. They are catching on fast.

In the first part of this book we'll tell you about these old ideas, which are new again. We'll tell you why a work center approach to kitchen design is the right approach for 21st century lifestyles. We'll focus on the centers that make a work center kitchen perform so well. We'll show you why they are the right ideas for larger kitchens and for kitchens that are part of larger, open greatroom spaces.

The second part of the book—the longer part—is a tour through twenty kitchens that demonstrate the ideas we talk about in part 1. We'll be speaking with the designers who put these ideas into practice for people just like you. Some of the homeowners will talk specifically about what they wanted and how they use the kitchens they got. What these designers and homeowners have today represents the latest thinking in work center kitchen design.

But kitchens are more than efficient space plans that make cooking and family activities easier. When we asked the twenty homeowners about what they wanted in their new kitchen, they all said they wanted to smile when they walked into it. That smile, day in and day out, was high on everyone's wish list. If seeing these kitchens makes you smile and if the kitchen you design for yourself as a result of this book makes you smile even more, then Nancy and I have accomplished what we set out to do.

Now let's get started with your new 21st century kitchen.

Contents

The Design Concept

In the 21st century, kitchens will be
designed to fit any lifestyle.
There will be specialized work
centers based on a new
approach to space planning—
one developed 60 years ago.

The 21st century kitchen was born at Cornell University in upstate New York in 1947. The ideas for it were developed by Mary Koll Heiner and Rose Steidl at the university's College of Home Economics. Their 1947 research and real-life testing was, as they said at the time, "directed toward integrating work centers in the kitchen to simplify the work performed there and to economize the use of the worker's [the cook's] body." They saw a functional kitchen as one that fit both the worker and the work to be done. They learned, through testing various kitchen layouts, that working in the kitchen could be made easier by the sensible arrangement of what they called "work centers." More testing showed that well-organized storage located at or near these work centers made them work even better. This was the beginning of what is now called "work center kitchen design."

So why look back; why this kitchen history? The answer is easy. What's old is new again. Work centers, the direct descendants of Heiner and Steidl's research, are what make the 21st century kitchen so versatile, so efficient and so adaptable to the demands we make on it. Knowing why and how work centers worked sixty years ago will help you understand why they will work for you today. We promise to keep this short, and there won't be a test.

Three Questions

Three questions motivated Heiner and Steidl in 1947: How can you arrange your kitchen to make your work easier? What are the things your family wants to do most in the kitchen? Do you want your kitchen to be a living kitchen—a room that is the shared activity center of the home? Sound familiar? Perhaps you've been asking yourself these same questions as you think about remodeling that old kitchen of yours. They are the basis of any wish list, the first step toward a new kitchen.

21st century kitchens
Understanding the Principles
of Work Center Design

Elements that make a
Work Center Kitchen work

The Food Storage Center localizes this function in a single one part of the kitchen A large refrigerator is positioned next to a walk-in pantry. The island has places to set-down grocery bags close to where things will be put away.

A Snack Center for the kids keeps them out of the cook's way. The microwave is near the freezer for quick and easy access to frozen foods. Putting it on this side of the kitchen makes it convenient for the kids to use, and close to the counter where they eat. A water cooler makes this snack center even more versatile.

A Casual Eating Area for the kids. This multi-use island gives them a place to eat and do homework. A divider separates their side of the island from the food preparation counter where their parents work.

The Cooking Center has a six burner commercial style cooktop with a cold water spigot to fill big pots on the spot. There is plenty of counter space on both sides of the cooktop, and the cook has close access to a butcherblock plating counter.

The Baking Center includes a marble countertop—the ideal material for rolling out pastry. The counter is lowered for less muscle strain and is close to both the ovens and and the prep sink. Customized drawers below the counter store supplies and utensils, much the same way they were stored in Hoosier cabinets 60 years ago,

The Fresh Food Prep Center, anchored by a prep sink, has plenty of work counter space for chopping foods and getting them ready for cooking. A pair of refrigerator drawers in base cabinets next to the sink stores fresh produce close to where it will be washed.

A high counter at the end of the island, gives both cooks a place where they can stand and browse through recipes.

The Clean-up Center is where the everyday dishes are stored in cabinets next to the kitchen's main dishwasher. Since it's next to the table where the family eats. these dishes are close to where they will be used.

13

Heiner and Steidl sought the answers through a series of tests using volunteers preparing typical meals. Results showed that kitchen tasks from preparation through cleanup were most efficiently handled by five task-specific work centers, which they ranked according to how often each was used. The sink center came in first since it was used for both food preparation and cleanup. Next came the range center. If you had a "two-piece range," which is what the primitive cooktops and wall ovens of the time were called, this became two centers: the oven center and the surface cooking center. Third was the mix center. Here was where you mixed, prepared, and assembled ingredients for meals; this included baking. The mix center took its cue from the Hoosier cabinet, the must-have accessory of its day. The Hoosier was the ultimate kitchen organizer. Packed into a single free-standing cabinet were bins used to store flour, sugar, and other staples. The bins were mounted above an enameled work surface. Spouts on the bins let the flour and sugar pour straight into bowls. Below the work surface was a drawer for utensils and, below that, cabinet space for storing pots, pans, pie plates, and bowls.

The refrigerator center and the china center tied for fourth. China centers provided storage for the dishes, silverware, and glasses used at the table. Remember, this was 1947, a time when dining rooms were used every day. Storing plates and serving pieces near the dining room table made sense.

First-use storage

Heiner and Steidl's research led to the principle of storing items close to where they are first used. Since the sink was the most important work center, they suggested that utensils needed for food preparation at the sink be stored near it. They called this area "sink first-use storage." In recommending what sort of utensils should be stored here and at other storage points in the kitchen, they gave preference to what was needed for the different tasks of food preparation at each work center: knives near where things were chopped, frying pans closer to the range, that sort of thing.

Watching the volunteer cooks work in the different test-kitchen layouts, Heiner and Steidl saw that most meals demanded moving regularly between the sink and range centers. Layouts that worked best had the sink and range positioned side by side or at right angles to each other. Either way, the cook could see what was cooking on the range from her position at the sink by just turning her head. Walking away from the sink wasn't necessary.

The location of the mix center depended on how the cook liked to work. One layout put it next to the sink; others placed it in between the sink and the range on the same wall, what we would call a galley kitchen today. The volunteer cooks found that they made more trips between the mix center and the sink than between the mix center and the range or between the mix center and the refrigerator.

Five or more appliances do not fit easily into small triangular spaces

Adding a second sink

None of these ideas are far removed from what we recognize today as the basics of good space planning for smaller kitchens. If Steidl's inquiries had stopped here, she would not have earned her place as the mother of modern kitchen design. But they didn't. In the mid 1950s, she tested an idea that would change how kitchens looked and worked. Steidl believed that for maximum efficiency, kitchens needed more than one sink. More tests with volunteer cooks proved this and led to suggested locations for the second sink.

These tests showed that a second sink was most useful in food preparation because it gave cooks a second water source—a place to clean and drain food and wash their hands. Test subjects found that the second sink tended to define the role of the primary sink as the

Two popular work centers in a 21st century kitchen are the snack center for kids, top, and a planning center for the parents, above. This snack center has a small wine cooler used to hold milk and juice. Both centers would be hard to fit into a work triangle kitchen.

Elements of the Work Triangle kitchen

The Work Triangle hasn't changed much in 65 years; what has changed is how we live

KITCHEN WORK TRIANGLE. CIRCA 1940

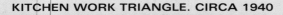

KITCHEN WORK TRIANGLE. CIRCA 2003

The basic work triangle kitchen was developed in the 1930s. Only three appliances counted: the sink, range and refrigerator. Back then, of course, only three appliances were available. Placing them in a triangular floor plan centralized food preparation and cooking tasks within the triangle.

The 1940s era kitchen is a cul-de-sac. No one can walk through the kitchen to hinder the cook working at her tasks. In the 2003 version, traffic has to move through the triangle to get to other places in the house, potentially disrupting kitchen efficiency.

Note the different counter heights in the 1940s kitchen—an idea that's just now being rediscovered. During the intervening years cabinet manufactures kept counter heights at a standard 36 inches, making the mass production of base cabinets more profitable.

cleanup center. The volunteers preferred a second sink near the range but couldn't see its usefulness when placed near the refrigerator. Steidl concluded that a second sink close to the range significantly improved the way a kitchen functioned—something we'd all agree with today. Steidl published her findings about second sinks in 1957 and 1961. Few people took any notice.

Work Triangles

The reason why people didn't notice was because of the kitchen work triangle—the other approach to kitchen design. Even though Heiner and Steidl showed that the typical early 1950s housewife appreciated those five work centers; and that Steidl independently proved the value of two sinks, the work triangle, with its single sink, became the standard for kitchen design. It remained so for forty years.

The thinking—actually the geometry—behind the work triangle goes something like this: Every kitchen has a range, a refrigerator, and a sink—just like Steidl's research kitchens at Cornell. These appliances are placed so that they form the points of a triangle. The legs of this triangle are the paths walked between the range, sink, and refrigerator during meal preparation. Efficiency in a work triangle kitchen is measured by the number of steps taken as you move about the triangle when preparing and cooking a meal. The fewer, the better.

The National Kitchen & Bath Association (NKBA), a proponent of kitchen work triangles and over the years the developer of the space-planning standards based on a triangular positioning of appliances, suggests that the maximum total distance of the triangle, the sum of the leg lengths, not exceed 26 feet. The group also says that no leg should be greater than 9 feet nor less than 4 feet. But kitchens are getting bigger, much bigger. Distances between cooking appliances, sinks, refrigerators—big kitchens often duplicate these appliances—and the other functional components in a large kitchen can easily exceed 9 feet. At what point does the triangle become so big that the kitchen is no longer an efficient place to work?

Mix centers, then and now. The Hoosier cabinet, top, with its convenient, task-specific storage was the prototype for today's baking center, above.

Problems with Work Triangles

Proponents of work triangle design don't have a good answer. This leads to some lively debates with designers who support work center space planning. The issues are not black and white; there is some common ground. The range in a work triangle kitchen does the same thing that it does in a work center kitchen. Both design approaches call this part of the kitchen the cooking center. The same thing with the sink—remember that a basic work triangle kitchen only has one—which in both systems is called the cleanup center.

Similarities stop here. In a work triangle kitchen, the refrigerator is considered a center—both the place for food storage and the anchor appliance for that part of the kitchen where food is prepared before it's cooked. By contrast, in a work center kitchen there is a specific area for food preparation, usually anchored by a second sink. In today's bigger kitchens, refrigerators are often

Islands are catalysts that make work center kitchens perform at their best

placed along the kitchen perimeter and are part of a storage wall, flanked by full-height cabinets, perhaps one of them a pantry. Taken together, this wall becomes the primary storage center in a work center kitchen.

What about that second sink that Steidl determined in 1957 to be so important to the efficiency of any kitchen? L-shaped and U-shaped kitchen layouts that create neat work triangles have no obvious place for it.

This isn't to say that the work triangle wasn't or isn't an efficient way to space-plan kitchens. It worked fine, as far as it went. Arranging the sink, range and refrigerator in an L-shape or U-shape layout, forming a proper triangle, automatically created plenty of storage

in the form of long runs of base cabinets with matching wall cabinets above. In these popular triangular layouts there was no need for walk-in pantries and Hoosiers. What they did was to create an expanding market for kitchen cabinet manufactures and a standardization of cabinets into stock sizes. Kitchen plans and counter lengths reflected the fact that base cabinets ranged from 12 to 48 inches in 3-inch increments. Everyone became comfortable with L-shape and U-shape layouts into which stock cabinet sizes fitted nicely.

New technologies

Then technology took a hand in kitchen design, starting with the microwave. When this originally bulky appliance shrank to where it could mount in a cabinet instead of having to sit on a counter or kitchen cart, it caught on as a must-have appliance. Designers, supported by manufacturers, quickly suggested that the best place for it was above the range—part of the cooking center. Over time, people began to see the microwave as a stand-alone appliance. They thought it should be closer to a freezer where it could be used to defrost meats or quickly cook prepared, frozen meals. Where was this place in a work triangle?

As families began to do everything in a hurry, the microwave came into its own as the cooking appliance that could best meet the "right now" attitude of kids, especially as every night sit-down family meals were little more than a memory. This led to the idea of the snack center. Where do you put this in a triangular layout?

What about a planning center? No one thought of this sixty years ago. Then, searching for recipes, writing shopping lists, or paying bills were done at a kitchen table or at a counter. Today, many people want a computer station in the kitchen so they can go online to shop. They want a desk for organizing all the paperwork that's part of being married with children. It has to fit somewhere, but where?

Planning centers, snack centers, food prep centers, and storage centers are what make 21st century kitchens work. So why did it take almost fifty years for work centers to catch on? One reason is that for

The evolution of islands

Islands started out as small tables that could be moved into the center of the kitchen where they could be used as food preparations areas allowing you to work sitting down

Today islands have evolved into important functional elements of the work center kitchen design. They provide locations for the second sink, like this island, and a specialized appliance—the wine cooler. There's also ample space for food preparation and eating. Note that the counter overhangs the island to create a knee space for the stools.

most of these years, kitchens were smaller and often separate rooms closed off by doors. There wasn't enough space for all these work centers, nor had the new appliances and convenience gadgets that required this additional space or at least a different approach to space planning to make them fit, been invented yet.

The kitchen work triangle was developed when there were only three appliances: the range—which included an oven below the surface cooking units—the refrigerator, and the sink. The dishwasher was just becoming popular. There were no refrigerator drawers, ice makers, or wine coolers; no dishwasher drawers, microwaves, or convection ovens. Now there are. Slavishly trying to fit five or six appliances, plus a second sink, into a layout formula originally designed for three can lead to frustration during the planning stage, and design mistakes that will come back to bite you when the project is done.

Lifestyle changes

Something else that held back implementation of work center design principles was a more traditional lifestyle that the baby boomers grew up in. Fathers worked; mothers stayed at home with the kids. Meals were eaten in the dining room; there were only four channels on the TV, and no video games. Computers hadn't been invented. Well, those days are gone. We are casual in everything we do; family members are always on the go, each needing to get things done and a place to do them.

In this on-the-go lifestyle, the kitchen is a grand central station for family activities of all kinds. This is

Pantries are another old idea coming back into vogue. The specialized storage spaces in the 1940s-era pantry, top, may surprise those who think this kind of specialization is brand new. Also back are butler's pantries, left. Once a sign of affluence in large homes with servants, today's version combines efficient storage with the additional counter space so useful when you entertain.

where the kids do their homework during the week, where you have friends over for supper on Saturday, and where you watch football on Sunday. If you need a family meeting, this is where it happens.

Cooking is no longer just a woman's work. Men cook—and like to. Kids cook, too. If you're having a party, several people could be cooking at once. In fact, having space for more than one cook is high on many wish lists. This means that space has to be found so that two people don't continually bump into each other. This space isn't usually inside the confines of a work triangle.

The walls come down

Both the original work triangle and Steidl's early work center kitchens envisioned a kitchen enclosed by four walls, with a door leading to a dining room and maybe a door leading to the outside. That's the way kitchens looked in the 1940s and 1950s, and these competing design approaches set out to make the best of the contemporary conditions.

Today, there are no partition walls. Kitchens are part of open living areas that include a place for casual eating and a family room. Often, there will be a home entertainment center focusing on a wide-screen TV. The dining room is pretty much a thing of the past. If used at all, it's only at the holidays: Thanksgiving, Christmas, or Passover.

Open plan kitchens, with their adjacent family rooms, great rooms, or casual living spaces led to the use of kitchen islands. Islands do important things.

They add useful counter space to the kitchen and provide an almost automatic location for a second sink, or cooktop closer to a sink—an arrangement of centers that reflects Steidl's idea that the cook shouldn't have to walk away from the sink in order to check on what's on the stove. Islands add storage space, cut down the walking distances between work centers, and establish traffic patterns that direct people easily through the kitchen and out of the cook's way.

Large islands function like big tables, providing room to eat or to put food out for buffet parties. They have lots of space for younger kids to do crafts or play games. For older ones, it's an after-dinner homework area—mom or dad, finishing cleanup chores, close by to answer questions. Islands are also natural room dividers. In open plans they are shared elements between rooms, with specialized storage on both sides. They are also a shared design element.

This brings us to the middle of the first decade of the 21st century and today's work center kitchen, the direct descendent of the work done by Steidl and Heiner. But first one more brief look back. A 1948 pamphlet written by Heiner, called *Functional Kitchen Storage*, has the following three suggestions on its first page: Build the cabinets to fit the woman. Build the shelves to fit the supplies. Build the kitchen to fit the family. Forgetting the politically incorrect language of the time, everyone planning a new kitchen today should keep these suggestions in mind. Helping you do that is what the next chapter is all about.

Build the cabinets to fit the cook.
Build the shelves for what you store.
Build the kitchen to fit the family.

Elements of Design

In the 21st century kitchen, work centers focusing on storage, lifestyle, personal style, and convenience for the kids will be just as important as the traditional cooking and cleanup centers.

23

We'll start by looking at the work centers that go into a 21st century kitchen: We'll see what they do, why they are important, and where they should go in your kitchen. Then we'll examine hidden elements of design that make 21st century kitchens so adaptable to today's lifestyle.

First the work centers.

How many work centers you want or need depends on how you use your kitchen, whether you have a family, and how old your children are. Ask yourself this, too: Do two people cook regularly? Is the kitchen a focal point for parties? How does it relate to the rooms around it? One thing is for sure, you'll want more than the five centers Steidl tested at Cornell sixty years ago. Because you'll certainly want at least two sinks—as Steidl suggested, the sink center is a good place to begin our kitchen tour.

Sink Centers

Their importance today is the same as it was in the 1940s. The primary sink, almost always the larger one, is used most for cleanup. The dishwasher goes next to it; together they form the cleanup center. The second sink is for food preparation: washing vegetables, filling cooking pots, a quick hands' wash, that sort of thing. The second sink should be located as close to the surface cooking units as possible. In this position, with plenty of countertop around it, it becomes the key element of your kitchen's food preparation center. To get the most out of a two-sink kitchen, plan the layout so the second sink anchors that food preparation area, and locate the sinks as far apart from each other as is practicable.

Cooking Centers

In a 21st century kitchen there can be one, or as many as three or four, cooking centers in task-specific locations. Commercial-style gas ranges are popular with people who like to cook. They provide six or eight burners, sometimes a grill and griddle combination, and one or two ovens. If this is what you want, and all you want, your kitchen will have a single cooking center. If you don't want a commercial-style range, or any range, the most common pairing is a cooktop and two wall ovens You can get the same high-power burners in a cooktop as you can with a commercial-style range.

Splitting your cooking appliances means that surface cooking can be done with gas, while baking and roasting are done in electric ovens. Serious bakers, who prefer the heat from an electric oven, are likely to want this. A wall oven often anchors a baking center that includes specialized storage, a marble counter to roll out dough and setdown space where just-baked items can cool down.

Ranges generally go against a wall because in this location it's easier to install the proper ventilation to exhaust heat, moisture and cooking odors. Grottoes that visually frame a commercial range against the rest of the kitchen are popular today. The grotto also hides the ventilation hood, which in a more traditional-looking kitchen, most people do not want to see. If you prefer a cooktop, efficient downdraft ventilation systems let you install the cooktop in an island and get the same exhaust power as from an overhead vent hood.

There are times when a task-specific cooking appliance—such as a gas wok burner or separate

Understanding the Elements
of Work center Design

electric steamer—solves a specific cooking problem. These specialized appliances, with their downdraft ventilation if required, are often on counters in other parts of the kitchen, away from the range or cooktop where they create another cooking center.

Food Preparation Centers

Picking the right location for the food preparation center, with its prep sink, is your first and most important space-planning task. Steidl's real-life testing showed that the preparation center should be close to the surface cooking area—steps away, perhaps right next to it. Chris Donner, a kitchen designer from Connecticut who designed one of the kitchens you'll see later on in this book, has a name for the area between these two centers. She calls it "the trench." This is where at least one cook spends most of his or her time, moving back and forth in it. Make sure the trench in your kitchen is out of the main traffic path that people take through the kitchen.

Refrigeration

In a 21st century kitchen, refrigeration won't always be in one location. It's no longer a point on a triangle. Large capacity refrigerators and freezers go where they are needed, sometimes split up and put at different ends of the kitchen. Refrigerators and freezers work in conjunction with other work centers rather than form

their own center. If you want only one refrigerator-freezer combination, put it outside the trench but easily accessible to where you cook and also where kids can get to it from another room without walking through the trench. That way workflow won't be interrupted by their comings and goings. Refrigerator drawers, beverage coolers, and ice makers mean that task-specific cooling can go exactly where it's needed. A refrigerator drawer, for example, near the prep sink is the right place to store fresh produce that will need to be washed. A freezer drawer near the microwave is the right spot for quick-cook frozen snack foods.

Planning Centers

We talked a bit about planning centers in Chapter 1—a work center never considered by either the early work triangle advocates or by Steidl and her Cornell colleagues. A well-thought-out planning center is the heart of the kitchen when it's not being used for cooking. A planning center belongs on the kitchen's perimeter; you should be able to reach it without walking through the kitchen.

The basic components are a desk area with an electrical outlet and a phone jack in the wall behind the desk, and a comfortable chair. The desk should be big enough for a computer screen or at least a laptop. Make sure that it has a shallow drawer for odds and ends and a deep one that can be used for filing. Your planning center can be a secondary home office, a place for

paying bills, organizing school events for the kids, or just a convenient place to go online when you need to check an airfare or make a bid on eBay.

Snack Centers

Another way to direct the kids away from the trench is to give them a snack center. Like refrigeration, snack centers belong on the kitchen perimeter. Well-equipped ones have a refrigerator drawer or an under-counter beverage cooler—they keep milk and juice just as cold and fresh as they keep beer and wine. The far side of a big island is a good location. So is a place in your kitchen that's close to a door leading outside. Another option is to put it close to where the kids watch TV or play videos. If your kids use a microwave to heat frozen snack foods, combining a microwave with a remote freezer drawer will give them what they need. Mounting a microwave used mostly by kids at their shoulder height is good safety feature.

Wetbars

Wetbars are small service areas away from the main kitchen area. They always include a small sink—the water source is what gives them their name—and are often accompanied by an ice maker. Sometimes a small under-counter refrigerator, a refrigerator drawer, or a wine cooler is included. In full service wetbars, you'll find a dishwasher.

Storage at the wetbar is usually customized for glassware and party supplies, with enough counter space to mix drinks and assemble hors d'oeuvres. For smaller gatherings, like a Sunday football afternoon with drinks, dry munchies, and popcorn, a wetbar can do everything the kitchen can and localize the mess.

While well-planned and well-positioned work centers give you a kitchen capable of meeting changing family and social needs, other important considerations affect both how it functions and how it looks. We call these the "hidden" elements of design, hidden because they are less noticeable and less likely to be written about. If noticed at all, it's because these elements aren't there. Causing you say to yourself, "Hey, something's missing here."

The rest of this chapter looks at these hidden elements: lighting, how to use color to unify a large open space that includes the kitchen and adjacent living areas, interesting new small appliances, and showing off your personality with collectibles. But we'll start with a design element that is hidden, in the truest sense of the word: good storage.

The number of **work centers** you have depends on how you use your **kitchen**

A wide array of customized storage options is available today—all aimed at keeping things where you need them. Deep drawers can be customized to hold pots or just their lids. Shallow drawers come with every kind of insert you can think of for storing silverware, kitchen knives, and utensils.

Mechanical inserts find space in formerly useless corner cabinets. Racks under cooktops hold large pots that seldom fit elsewhere, and 6-inch wide pull-outs can hold everything from spices to dish towels.

Storing the Stuff
Where you use it first

Having enough storage won't be a problem in the 21st century kitchen. Bigger kitchens will automatically provide the space you need. More important is how storage can be organized so you won't be running all over to find what you need.

Which brings us back to the Heiner and Steidl's principle of storage based on the point of first use. Simply put, this means that pots and pans should be stored near the surface cooking units, knives and measuring cups near the food prep areas, and dishes close to where you plate your meals. For real efficiency, dish and glassware storage should also be close to a dishwasher. Keep snack foods close to where you want your kids to eat them—or hope they will eat them. If there are two cooks in your kitchen, don't hesitate to double up on key items—two sets of knives if there are two prep areas, or a prep area and a baking center.

Think through your storage requirements before you buy the cabinets. Make a list of what you need to put away and decide where you want to put it.

Efficient storage isn't limited to what's kept behind closed doors. The glass jars, top, holding all sorts of staples are eye-catchers. When placed near a prep counter, their contents are conveniently available when needed as ingredients.

More often, special storage solutions are built into places designed to accommodate them. Movable drawer pegs, above, can be arranged to hold different dish sizes, while curved shelves in an end cabinet, right, are perfect for storing large bowls.

Big pantries are returning to kitchens now that kitchens are large enough to have them. There are two kinds:

Butler's pantries are open, separate rooms off the kitchen, usually with counters for food preparation or serving buffets. Sometimes they have a sink, dishwasher, refrigerator, or a warming drawer. Bulter's pantries often connect the kitchen to an eating area or dining room.

Walk-in pantries are like walk-in closets. They have customized shelf storage, though seldom any appliances, and can always be closed off by a door.

Storing the Stuff
In pantries

In the 21st century, storage of staples and other non-perishables will be centralized in pantries—a return to an idea popular until the 1950s, before they gave way to long cabinet runs. Pantries are back in fashion because they hold a lot, are easy to organize, and because there is a trend away from using wall cabinets—and the stuff has got to go somewhere. A basic pantry is like a small closet with adjustable shelves, often built-in on one side of the refrigerator.

Pullout pantries—full-height, base cabinet height or some height in between—are options all cabinet manufacturers offer. Their shelf arrangements can be customized to maximize the space behind the door and make the stored items easy to see and reach from both sides of the open pantry.

Putting Things Away

● Store cooking utensils and dishes close to where you first use them.

● If you are left-handed, store your most used utensils where you reach for them with your left hand.

● Heavy items in wall cabinets should be no higher than your shoulders; in base cabinets, no lower than your knees.

● Heavy cooking pots are best stored in drawers directly under the cooktop. If you cook on a range, keep the pots in drawers or on shelves right next to it.

● High shelves in wall cabinets or pantries are the right places for seasonal items.

● Put a refrigerator drawer near a sink to store produce that has to be washed.

Unconventional displays **create spectacular effects. The collection of antique storage tubs, above, sits on glass shelves hung from a pipe, itself suspended from the ceiling.**

Personalize your kitchen.

You're in your kitchen a lot, so you might as well have things around you that you enjoy: a tea cup collection, travel souvenirs, antique pots, anything that expresses your personality; it doesn't matter. Glass door cabinets are a great place to display these items that show off your personality.

These displays should not, however, take away space needed to store things used regularly. Creating nice display spaces is an important part of a good storage plan. That's why you should consider it together with other storage questions.

Cabinet manufacturers sell wall units that make displaying things easy. These have full glass doors and three or more shelves (sometimes glass themselves) to show off your collectibles. Often, the cabinet roof can accommodate a "puck light" for illuminating displayed items. If you want to combine storage with display—a polite way of saying that you may not want to worry about seeing perfectly styled stacks of plates and soup bowls behind glass doors—you can pick a cabinet door that is solid on the lower two-thirds and glass on top.

Let your **kitchen** show off your **personality**

Think of light as layers of brightness that shine throughout the kitchen

A well-lit kitchen must combine three sources of light in an integrated plan. In the 21st century, the best plan is one that uses these separate sources to create a layered effect with light.

The top layer is called the ambient light source. It provides the general illumination for your kitchen. In older kitchens this was a centrally located light fixture. That caused a problem: the single light cast a shadow over whichever counter you worked at. Today, ambient lighting should come from several recessed ceiling lights arranged to light the whole room evenly and reduce counter shadows.

The second layer is task lighting, a critical one for ease of work. Task lighting focuses light on your work centers: the sinks, the range, and the food preparation counters. Task lighting is best handled by recessed down lights aimed at the work areas and controlled by a switch that is separate from the one that turns on your ambient lighting.

A big change today is that high-intensity, low-voltage lights have replaced under-cabinet fluorescent lights as the source for task lighting. Low-voltage light shines a bright white light that's easy to work under and is easy on the eyes.

Islands and peninsulas need their own light sources. Pendant lights, either ceiling-mounted or hanging from a monorail, are good choices here. Make sure to put them on a dimmer.

The third layer of light is accent lighting. This is light for drama, not for functional illumination: light on displayed objects or light that visually balances a room top to bottom, valance lighting near the ceiling, or a strip of low-voltage rope lights under a toe kick creating a warm glow on the floor are examples of this.

The trend in lighting today is a low-voltage monorail system from which pendant lights of various lengths and wattages hang down to light various parts of the kitchen. This system lets you combine ambient light (the lights close to the ceiling) with task lighting (the low-hanging pendants). Monorail systems also combine easily with traditional incandescent decorative pendants.

Traditional pendant lights, available in a wide range of styles, are good choices to install above smaller islands. By putting your kitchen lighting on dimmers, you can brighten the light for working or dim it for mood lighting.

Light the Right Way

● You can never have enough light, so be generous with your lighting plan. You can always turn off what you have; but you can't turn on what isn't there.

● Go beyond the minimum number of lighting circuits specified by the building code. Divide your ambient and task lighting between three or four separately-controlled circuits.

● Put all of your ambient lighting on dimmers.

● Display lighting should always be on its own circuit separate from either task or ambient lighting.

● When selecting non-recessed fixtures or pendant lights, choose models that are easy to clean and have easy access for changing bulbs.

Here is a sampling of appliances that goes beyond cooktops and ranges. These task-specific appliances make it possible to have more than one cooking center.

Wok burners, right, have a single, high output gas burner with a grate designed to hold a curved wok.

Modular cooking units, next to wok burner, that supplement the range or cooktop include vegetable steamers, deep fryers, and single burners with 15,000 or more BTUs of heat output. Install them separately, or as a group, to form another cooking center.

Counter-mounted grills, opposite page top center, provide year-round barbecue at a moment's notice. New types of downdraft vents have been developed to remove smoke, moisture, and odor.

The cook sink, opposite page top right, fills and drains like any other sink but it also cooks. Use it for boiling pasta, for steaming, or to slow-cook soups and stews.

Dishwashers, like refrigerators, now come in drawer units, opposite page center right, that can be installed where you need them.

Appliances your mother never dreamed of

Welcome to 21st century kitchen technology. It has come a long way in a few years, pushed along by all of us who like to cook.

Most of the really neat stuff is for cooking—not fancy ranges or cooktops, but small, counter-mounted appliances for specialized cooking tasks you might not want to do on a range or cooktop. Refrigerator and freezer drawers let you store fresh produce at the preparation center: juice, milk, and soda at the snack center, and frozen meals near the microwave.

For cleanup chores there are dishwasher drawers. Smaller than traditional dishwashers, they can be put right where you need them: close to the range to wash pots, close to the prep sink to wash mixing bowls and utensils, or at the snack center to take care of the kids' dirty dishes.

The biggest change in appliance design is that microwaves are now made as pull-out drawers, something that should please left-handers tired of reaching in from the right.

Where to Put Them

- Steamers, cook sinks, and deepfryers can be mounted in any counter. Plan a second, smaller cooking center around them.
- Wok burners and similar cooking appliances should be close to the cooktop or range so they can be vented by a single hood. If located elsewhere, they will need separate venting.
- Refrigerator drawers are best placed near your food preparation center or, if used to keep cold soda for the kids, near the snack center
- A freezer drawer is usually paired with a refrigerator drawer. Since both drawers will probably be near the prep center, plan to locate your microwave close by and use the freezer drawer to store heat-and-eat convenience meals.
- A dishwasher drawer makes sense near a range or cooktop where it can be used to wash small loads of pots, pans, and cooking utensils. Another good place is at the wet bar, where it can handle party glasses and snack plates

Color is the best tool to integrate a kitchen into the rooms around it. Color makes all rooms warm and inviting and it helps create balance. While paint is the best and fastest way to add color, fabrics also play a part.

For big open-plan spaces, choosing one color for all of the walls will give you the unity you want. Painting large areas in various colors can be jarring to the eyes. There are exceptions. In some big, open-plan spaces, some people like the kitchen to loudly proclaim itself as "The Kitchen." Within a kitchen, contrasting colors or finishes between the cabinets and an island can add both visual impact and visual separation.

The best way to define space and the activities planned for them is with furniture. Think of an island with several bar stools around it as a furniture grouping. Rugs do the same thing. A rug near a lesser-used work center along the edges of the kitchen—a planning center or wetbar center—makes a nice design statement and sets that center off from others in the kitchen. But a rug in the kitchen trench area isn't a good idea. It's too easy to trip over and very likely to get dirty.

Color draws the eye to what you want people to see. The progression of color from red to yellow, above, moves the eye from the kitchen to a scaled-down eating and work area for small children. Alternatively, the bright red cooking center, below, immediately catches the eye and announces that this is the most important part of this kitchen.

Color and texture will unify the open rooms that radiate around the kitchen

The Coloring Book

● Using the same fabric or color scheme in the kitchen and the rooms around it will unify the space.

● If you want white cabinets, think about putting them against a colored wall to create eye-catching interest.

● Painting a small room next to the kitchen a different color will define that room as having a different use.

● Color is subjective. Forget about the old saw that light colors make small rooms seem larger while darker ones hem it in. If a bright color will make you smile, use it.

Putting all the elements together

Before looking at how twenty people, individuals and families, just like you, used the ideas behind work center kitchen planning and the elements of design we've just talk about, a few words about how people in different parts of the country approach kitchen design are appropriate. We asked three designers, whose work is shown in this book, to talk about this.

Connecticut designer Donner notes that East coast kitchens tend to be large. We found them to be larger than those we saw in other parts of the country. Perhaps because of their size, they are very family-oriented, with places for kids to work, play, or help with cooking. They are also animal-friendly. Given their size, the first item on the design list is where to put the work trench—a term Donner uses frequently to define where the cook works. This comes before planning traffic-flow patterns through-out the kitchen.

Midwest kitchens are a bit smaller. One of the main concerns of her clients, according to Maureen O'Neil from Abruzzo Kitchens in Chicago, is disguising the appliance fronts, making them look like part of the cabinetry. We saw this in Cincinnati, too. But not so much in the East, where people want high-tech stainless steel appliances to create a sharp contrast to their traditional tastes in cabinet styles. The smaller Midwest kitchens mean, too, that work centers sometimes change functions. For example, a snack center used by the kids during the day, can turn into a place where drinks are served before a dinner party

This is what Julie Young, CKD, from Carmel Kitchens in California, likes to call a beverage zone—a place in the kitchen for adults to be in the kitchen, but out of the way while the cooks work. Two of our smaller kitchens come from the West coast. Both had a perch zone—another term Young likes to describe her approach to getting the most out of a smaller space.

Now it's time to put all the theory into practice. We invite you to tour the twenty kitchens shown in the next four chapters. We hope that what we show you helps when the time comes to put theory into practice in your own kitchen.

A word about terms

We use three terms throughout this book that we want to summarize for you, to avoid any confusion, since some of them appear to be used interchangeably.

Work Centers. Hopefully, you know this one already. These are the areas of the kitchen where different task are done—cooking, preparing, clean-up, snacking, going on line.

The Work Trench. This is the area where the cook spends most of his or her time. It comprises an area bounded by the cooktop or range, the food preparation center and at least one sink. The work trench should be placed so that no one needs to walk through it while the cook is working.

Work Zones. These are areas where two or more close-together work centers combine to make kitchen tasks easier. For example, the food preparation, cooking and cleanup centers together form a cooking zone.

3

Family Kitchens

The kitchen is the heart of the home;
it has always been so. In the 21st
century, kitchens will expand
and become the welcoming
focal point of family life and a
family-oriented lifestyle.

Raising Arizona

In 1936, kitchens were small; they were shut away behind closed doors, and if you had the means, your hired cook was the only person who used it. Not a setup for modern family living. In Tucson, Arizona, however, these older houses had historical significance and architectural features dating from what locals call the Arizona territorial period. Keeping these features and the charm that came with them was, and still is, important when planning a remodeling in Tucson.

This Tucson house fits that bill. The owners were still coping with the effects of the first kitchen remodeling done in 1949, which was not an improvement on the original layout. It still had just the basic appliances and a few feet of counter space crammed into a 10 × 11-ft. kitchen that also had to accommodate an eating table. The little kitchen was stuck between the maid's quarters—they didn't have one—and the rest of the house.

More countertop space is the biggest addition to this new kitchen. The owners chose soapstone tops to create a rough-hewn contrast to the glossy wall tiles. The peninsula that separates the kitchen from the eating area is topped in butcher block, both to reduce any chance that those soapstone counters would read as one black monolith, and to unify it with the floor.

Then they decided to start their family and things had to change. In addition to the maid's quarters—also about 10 feet square—the area behind the kitchen had a laundry room, also about 10 feet square. Expanding beyond the footprint of the original house was out of the question. The space they needed would be cobbled together for three small, square rooms.

Kameron Rutschman of Dorado Designs in Tucson worked out the plan for them. Her design tripled the space available, but the resulting kitchen was long and somewhat narrow—too narrow for an island but too wide for an efficient galley layout. Rutschman's solution was a small peninsula for the food preparation center. Close to the range, this peninsula layout follows Steidl's recommendation that one sink be positioned so that the person working at it can see what's cooking on the range by just turning his or her head.

The peninsula breaks the space into two rooms, eliminating what could have been the bowling-alley effect of a single 28-foot-long by 11-foot-wide open space. It's close to both the refrigerator and a small pantry, provides a set-down area for foods coming out of the microwave, and is a handy serving counter for people eating casual meals at the table.

What's striking about this kitchen are the warm yellow wall tiles and the vibrant colors of

At 10 × 11 feet the old kitchen, inset, wasn't much: a sink under a window, the range on the adjacent counter with a 30-inch cabinet for separation, a refrigerator at the end of the other counter, plus a dishwasher added at the expense of a storage cabinet.

The new kitchen has more than triple the space. It also has the sink—enlarged and improved—under the same window, the only one on that side of the house.

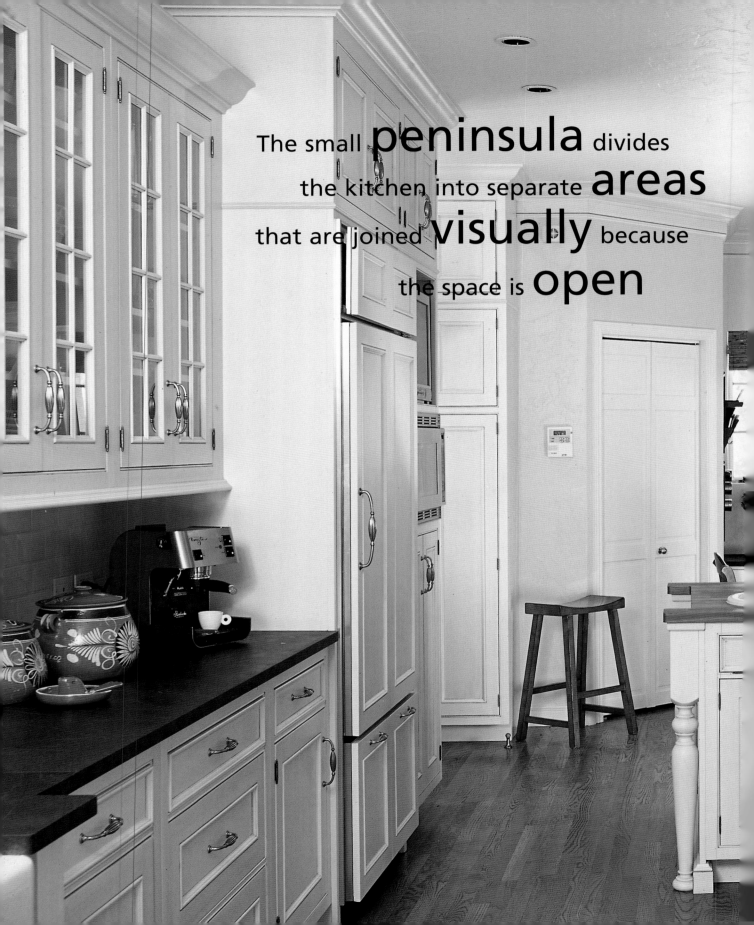

The small **peninsula** divides the kitchen into separate **areas** that are joined **visually** because the space is **open**

the Mexican Talavera pottery on display. The owners had been collecting it for years; some of it was in the old kitchen. Rutschman re-used the old kitchen's display technique—deep shelves above the windows where the pottery could sit securely. To create what looks like a single, continuous display area, she built a shelf out from the chase hiding the range hood ducts. Window treatments are simple: matchstick blinds formed into Roman shades. She didn't want anything to compete with the Talavera. For the same reason, there is only one cabinet on this display wall.

Niches chiseled out of brick walls are common in Tucson. The one added behind the range is similar to others elsewhere in the house dating from the original construction. Both Rutschman and the owners saw it as a big, tactile focal point. And unlike the shallow kitchen niches built with wood frame construction, the double brick walls in the Southwest are deep enough to be used as open storage spaces. That was important here, since there are no wall cabinets close to the range.

Shallow, open shelves give the owners a place for books and a few more pieces of Mexican pottery. This is a compromise in a kitchen with a cabinet-free wall. While the window shelf impedes access to the books, the alternative would have been no book storage at all.

A well-organized and compact planning center, left, is tucked into an alcove behind the eating table—a good use of space that might have gone unused otherwise. A small corner room holds the new laundry.

Only a round table, below left, could easily fit in the space that Rutschman allowed for an eating area. Space had to be left for people coming through the back door and for access to the laundry room. The 30s-era art deco light fixture above the table previously hung in the dining room.

Positioned flush with the cabinets, the TV, below right, swivels so it can be seen from anywhere in the kitchen.

Channel Islands

A great kitchen is like a conversation:

straight-talking and attentive-listening on both sides, resulting in agreement. The conversation here between Cincinnati architect Mark McConnell and his client shows how the design process should work in the 21st century. The client—I'll call her Linda—doesn't want her real name used. Her existing kitchen wasn't small, but the space-planning, while efficient for one cook, didn't work when other family members wanted to use the kitchen at the same time. Everyone ended up all jumbled up in a corner. "My goal was to have space for other people to work, but for me to be separated from them," Linda recalled. "When I'm cooking I don't like others to be where the mess is."

She explained this to McConnell, who had been brought in to design an addition for the new kitchen. Initially, McConnell was not

Two islands, with a 24-inch aisle between them, link together work centers on both sides of the kitchen. Two prep centers, each with its own sink, let two cooks work easily. The primary prep center is self-contained on the smaller island. The smaller sink on the big island serves the cook at the range, while the round table on the island's end is the everyday eating area.

the kitchen designer. That changed once they started talking.

McConnell picks up the story: "Homeowners like Linda have a feeling in mind of what they want, but aren't trained to draw their dream on paper. We show up at the first meeting with pencils and tracing paper. The client starts talking and we start drawing. Right on the spot the client can say, 'yes, you've got it,' or 'no, not like that.' We keep sketching until what's in the client's mind begins to appear on paper."

When McConnell's pencil had finished drawing, Linda's ideas looked like this: a prep area with a refrigerator drawer to keep fresh produce close to the sink where it will be washed, a commercial-style range with a second sink nearby for additional prep tasks, and a microwave cooking area with a close-at-hand freezer drawer for the frozen meals her kids could heat up when they were in a hurry. The dishwasher and trash compactor are in their traditional spots next to the sink, turning this area into a double-duty work center—both prep and cleanup.

Space for the new kitchen came from a 13-foot addition bump out from a bay window in the old kitchen. It provided enough room for a large island with an attached round "table" for eating and a long work counter running almost to the sink wall at the other end of the kitchen.

But the big island caused a problem. "I

A coffee area in the dining room with a bar sink and a dishwasher drawer gives the owners a separate place for preparing, serving and cleaning up light snacks. The planning center, on the other side of the door, is designed with a trash area below the desk so that junk mail can be disposed of quickly.

realized that I would have to walk completely around the island to get to the refrigerator on the other side." That's Linda recalling her first look at it during construction. McConnell hadn't seen it on the drawings; neither had she. The solution was to divide the island in two, separating the halves with a 2-foot pass-through. This made a path—the shortest distance between two points, so says the definition—from one side of the kitchen to the other, and linked the range to the microwave. The division also clearly marked the smaller island as the main food preparation center.

At this point, Cincinnati kitchen designer and cabinet maker Kimball Derrick joined the conversation. His role was to suggest and build kitchen storage cabinets, plus specialized ones in the casual dining room that met two family needs. The first was the coffee bar, designed because Linda likes to entertain friends over coffee. This is easily done with the dishewasher and sink Derrick built in the unit. For something stronger than coffee, there's also a wine cooler.

Nothing could be done about a door leading out of the kitchen. It created a continuity problem since Derrick wanted wall units on both sides of the door. No need for additional storage or another appliance there, but it was an obvious place for a planning center. The one he put there is out of the ordinary. It's designed for people to work standing up. Linda calls it the "man tower." Her husband uses it to open and dispose of mail. Inside the base cabinet is a recycling center: the waste paper doesn't have to travel far.

▶ To Your Kitchen

From the Designer

TALK THROUGH EVERYTHING before you start. It's better than being surprised later on, and finding yourself screaming the words, "I wish I had thought of that." **BE FLEXIBLE** and open to change. If you see during construction that changes are needed, don't be afraid to make them. **LEAVE ENOUGH COUNTER SPACE** on both sides of your range to set down hot pans. This is even more important when a hearth encloses the cooking area and separates it from the rest of the countertop. **REFRIGERATOR DRAWERS** take pressure off the main refrigerator by providing storage for frozen snacks and cold beverages for the kids.

The microwave, opposite page, has its own work center, on the other side of the island—out of the trenches so the kids can use it without interfering with the cook.

A casual dining room, left, is just beyond the big island. The table, along with the coffee station, provides a large buffet area for family meals.

The primary sink, below left, positioned across from the refrigerator drawers, does double duty, serving as a prep sink for the second cook.

The commercial-style range, below right, sits under a hearth that hides the ventilator. Pull-outs on either side of the hearth store spices and condiments.

Eyes for the Past

Growing up in Ireland, your ideas about kitchens differ from those of Americans. For one thing, you probably are comfortable with an older look—not a modern-day interpretation of country this or country that, but the timeless elegance of Georgian style that continues to influence design in the British Isles to this day. And when you visualize the kitchen you want, you may see it as groupings of furniture-like pieces rather than runs of base cabinets with wall cabinets above them—what Europeans call an unfitted kitchen look.

Now your home is in Connecticut and that old, remembered look is what you want for your new family kitchen over here. And you like to cook.

The owners of this kitchen began recreating this unfitted look by first hiring a friend who is a retired architect. His plan added a 150-square-foot space to the back of the house, which is where the

The island with a mahogany **top is the center of family activity and where the kids sit to help with cooking. The mahogany has been treated with a marine-quality finish to protect it from moisture. Behind the island, to the right of the ovens, is the 48-inch-wide storage pantry. It's made to look like an armoire, in keeping with the European feel the owners wanted.**

new kitchen would be. His straightforward layout called for splitting cooking and baking functions between two centers, on opposite sides of the kitchen: an island for food preparation and eating, and a planning center in a transitional space between the kitchen and the new breakfast room. It was a good plan, but to those Irish eyes looking at the elevation drawings, it was too contemporary—too many runs of base cabinets with too many wall cabinets above them. Not at all a look recalling the memory of an old country kitchen.

That's when they turned to Connecticut designer Chris Donner. The owners were clear, Donner remembers: they liked the floorplan and nothing on it would be altered. But they wanted the look changed. Donner did this by suggesting material the owners hadn't thought of: soapstone counters, a mahogany top for the island, subway tiles with a rough, crackle finish. Then she showed them how these materials could be combined with warm wood cabinets made and placed to look like furniture.

Donner began at the island. It was functional and centrally placed but looked like a big box in the center of the kitchen. She suggested giving it an Edwardian look with wainscotted sides, painted off-white to contrast with the cabinets. Adding the mahogany top, the decorative brackets, and bun feet make the island look like a piece of furniture.

Varying colors and textures, from the island sides in wainscotting, to the subway tiles used to surround the range, to the open areas on the wall, give this kitchen the European unfitted look the owners were after. For a bit of whimsy in this Georgian kitchen, they commissioned a very modern kinetic sculpture to hang over the island, which they like to watch turn in the wind.

A different kind of foot—more accurately called furniture cut-out toes—was specified for the cooktop cabinet. Its shelves for pot storage were left open to provide a visual break from the wood-fronted base cabinets on either side of it. Cut-out toes were also used on the sink cabinet. And the only two wall cabinets got glass doors with Georgian mullion bars.

Storage in this kitchen is centralized in a 48-inch-wide, ceiling-height pantry. Donner's decorative touches made it look more like an armoire—eighteenth-century pilasters frame it and the new fronts trick the eye into thinking there are four doors instead of two.

The planning center is next to the storage pantry. The owner had cookbooks she wanted to see; she also had old magazines and school directories she didn't want to see. So Donner designed the center with open shelves directly above the desk for the books and closed cabinets for everything else. In addition to the desk, an old-fashioned pull-out breadboard above the filing drawers provides extra space for laying out bills—but only when needed. One feature in the planning center, not seen often, is a set of cubbies, rather like message boxes in a roll-top desk. There's one for each family member, six of them plus a spare, which, the owner jokes, doesn't indicate that she is about to have another child.

The irregular surfaces on the subway tiles Donner used on the backsplashes and the curved surround over the cooktop—a handmade crackle finish—pick up the pinks, violets, and browns from elsewhere in the kitchen. Inserted into this crackle-finish field tile behind the cooktop are two tile murals designed to look like medieval woodcuts—a design idea that harks back to the eighteenth century.

▶ To Your Kitchen

BUN FEET ON ISLANDS and toe cut outs on base cabinets will give both the look and feel of furniture. **WOOD COUNTERS** are beautiful, but they need to be treated and sealed. A marine finish works best for mahogany and teak. Ask about what's best for other woods. **SOAPSTONE COUNTERS** create a wonderful textural contrast and they wear well. But the only color they come in is black.

The breakfast room, below left, is in the space where the original kitchen used to be.

Contrasting with the black soapstone counters, a white farm sink, far left and opposite, anchors the kitchen's cleanup center.

Pull-out shelves next to the dishwasher, left, are placed at kid height—setting the table and doing the dishes are their jobs. These dish shelves are also near where the family eats.

Seven cubbies built into the planning center, below right— one for each family member, plus a spare—keep family activities organized.

Family Planning

Something for everyone: an admirable goal seldom achieved. That probably makes the goal of giving everybody everything even more remote. It needn't be that way in kitchen design. This Minneapolis kitchen, which is shown in Chapter 1, proves that a functionally perfect design is possible.

You can talk about this kitchen in terms of this or that work center, but its most interesting feature is that the spaces, zones, and centers for the kids are as important as those for the cooks, and they are planned with the same attention to detail.

Tricia Hauser Tidemann at Northstar Kitchens in Minneapolis designed this kitchen and remembers it as a challenging project, a true collaboration between her and the owners, proving again that one plus one often equals three. The owners, Wade and Nancy, both engineers and good cooks, gave Hauser a fifteen-page list of things they wanted for sure or wanted to consider as possibilities.

Here is an ideal cooking center for a great amateur chef who likes to prepare restaurant-quality meals for his family and gourmet fare for church suppers. Open drawers below the cooktop keep pots and pans close and visible. Hanging utensils are within easy reach, and there are set-down areas on both sides. Directly behind the cooktop is a counter used for plating.

A very short sampling from that list includes:

Prep center counters that are 3 inches below bent-elbow height (taking into account the shoes typically worn). This sets them higher than the normal 36 inches;

Three feet of room for the first person at the food preparation center, with an additional 2 feet for each additional person. This center, as they built it, has room for three;

A faucet at the prep sink that can be controlled with the elbow or the back of the hand when the hands are grungy from working with food.

Several more pages outlined how and where they wanted to store things ranging from a mortar and pestle, to sponges, to bags of potatoes.

Making all this work required a lot more space, plus exceptional—not just good—organization. The space came from Wade and Nancy's unused dining room, the typical place to find space in houses built during the 1970s. Expanding into the dining room gave Hauser a 15 × 20 ft. area to work with—plenty of space for the long island that makes the design work. The eight work centers in this kitchen are discussed at length on pages 12 and 13. We'll focus here on how the island provides everything Wade, Nancy and their two kids needed and wanted.

First the kids. Nine feet of the island belong to them. More important, a vertical divider separates their side of the island from the long food prep center. Messes on both sides stay put. From where the kids sit, it's an easy reach to the microwave and to get hot or cold water from the cooler. They are also close to the refrigerator, if they want milk or

Talk about a big island that does everything—a far cry from the little square thing, inset, in the old kitchen. The two-chair snack bar is for the kids; the vertical island divider keeps their things from overflowing onto the food preparation counter. But it's not all function. Opposite the island, next to the baking center, is a display cabinet for things that are seen, but not used.

The split island defines a
snack center and a
prep area

The cleanup center, right, which the owners call their wet zone, is at the far end of the kitchen—away from the prep and cooking centers, but right next to the dining room and the dirty dishes.

Looking ahead to a time when the owners are older, and perhaps shorter, they requested a foot stool, below, that hides away in a toe kick. Though the owners do not use it much now, they realize that the time will come when they will need the foot stool to reach the higher shelves.

Separated from the working side of the kitchen and close to the microwave and refrigerator is the kids' very own snack and work area, below right.

juice, and to the freezer for microwavable munchies—all the time well away from the areas where Wade and Nancy cook and bake. But this is more than a snack center. The long counter is ideal for craft projects, playing games and—oh yes—doing homework.

The other three sides of the island serve the business of cooking and baking, starting with a bookcase for cookbooks and recipe folders. Its raised counter is the right height for someone who wants to work standing up. At the opposite end is a lowered butcher-block counter used by Wade to plate food coming off the cooktop. The couple's good dishes are kept here in customized plate drawers.

The preparation counter is restaurant-grade stainless steel—nothing better when it comes to hygiene. Though the kitchen has a walk-in pantry, many of the nonperishable staples are kept in bins and drawers below this counter. There is also a refrigerator drawer for fresh produce. Positioning the prep sink at a junction between the prep counter, the cooking center, and the baking center means that no one is more than a step or two away from water.

The modern baking center **is a descendant of the Hoosier Cabinet. Everything needed for pies, cakes, and cookies is here. The lowered marble counter is the right surface for rolling out dough. Drawer and cabinet storage is customized for what will be stored there, and the ovens are close at hand.**

▶ To Your Kitchen

From the Designer

WRITE DOWN EVERYTHING you want on your wish list; there is no such think as a wish list that's too short. **THINK ABOUT A DESIGN** that plans for future needs—when your kids get older and when you do, too. **LOCATING THE CLEANUP** center close to the eating area is a good idea, but make sure there is a second sink near the food preparation and cooking centers.

Western Casual

Right away it's obvious that this is a casual, family place. We aren't asked to take our shoes off. The slate floor in the kitchen and throughout the first floor is to be used, we are told, not just looked at. While we are there, the couple's two girls—seven and nine—drive past the kitchen island on push scooters.

The owners share their kitchen story with us. They met in a parking lot. Casual conversation quickly turned into a next-day meeting at Starbucks with both their families: her young girls, his older boys. A week later on the first date, he asked her if she'd be willing to design his new kitchen. A year later that kitchen is the gathering point for the extended families.

She knew what she wanted; she cooked. He just wanted an informal, easy-to-live-in kitchen with a place set aside to make coffee. Jim Dase, CKD, from Abruzzo Kitchens in Schaumberg, Illinois, working with Maureen O'Neil as project manager, helped

Reflecting a 21st century trend, the kitchen has only one wall cabinet—at the cooking center. Moving storage off the wall to base cabinets is better ergonomically, even in smaller kitchens. It allows exterior walls to be used for windows. The in-counter cook sink—a second cooking center—next to the prep sink cooks pasta, corn or lobsters, or can be a Crock-Pot for soups.

Ovens at both ends of the counter create **Visual symmetry**

The cooking center, right, illustrates the principle of first-use storage: Frying pans are kept in the shallow drawers; heavy pots and pans go in the deep ones.

Designed as a fine piece of furniture, a wall unit, below left, at the far end of the kitchen, hides the refrigerator, two freezer drawers, and a pantry. To the right of it is the coffee station, which the owners—big coffee drinkers—insisted on.

A commercial-style faucet at the cleanup sink, opposite page bottom, is handy for cleaning dirty pots too large to fit into the dishwasher.

▶ To Your Kitchen

DEEP DRAWERS BELOW THE COOKTOP keep pots and pans at the point of first use and eliminate bending or reaching for them. **A COOK SINK,** steamer, or other in-counter appliance creates an instant, secondary specialized cooking center and a comfortable place to sit and eat. **WANT PERFECTLY HYGIENIC COUNTERS?** Consider an engineered stone or quartz counter. They offer better protection against bacteria than other counter materials. **LAMINATE CABINETS** are easily repaired with photographically-exact duplicates of any door or drawer front that's been damaged.

both of them get it all. For a complete remodel, the space allotted for the new kitchen turned out to be long, narrow and not that large. Work triangle space-planning could have been used, but it wouldn't have been able to handle the seven work centers that Dase had planned for them. Here's what had to fit: two cooking centers, a microwave snack center, a baking center, a food preparation center, plus cleanup and coffee areas—enough to provide unlimited possibilities for family members to use the kitchen any way they chose.

Dase put the cooktop on a partition wall to the right of the long sink counter. He skewed it off center to the right—a perfect example, O'Neil says, of form following function. With this asymmetrical arrangement, one person can cook while the other has plenty of counter space to prepare the food. The cooktop is close to the wall oven—one of two—that's used for meal preparation. The microwave is directly across from it mounted at a height convenient for the kids.

It's the other cooking center that gets the most use—the one by the cook sink. This in-counter appliance boils water, steams vegetables, or cooks anything that can be cooked in a pot. It fills from the prep sink faucet next to it but has its own drain, like any sink. Dase put it in the island so the family can pull up stools and use it like a fondue pot. As a slow cooker, it makes ready-to-eat healthy snacks for the kids just home from school.

The counters are kid-friendly, too: man-made nonporous engineered stone that's impervious to germs and bacteria, unlike many other counter materials. Their iridescence contrasts with the high-gloss cabinets done in faux cherry laminate— a photographic process that creates exact, simulated wood grain. The original grain pattern photos are kept by the manufacturer so if a cabinet is damaged, an exact duplicate of the damaged piece can be ordered as a replacement.

4

Kitchens for Parties

Kitchens go public when you entertain.
In the 21st century, kitchens will be
flexible enough to move effortlessly
and quickly from being the focus
of family activities to the
life of the party.

Entertain Anytime

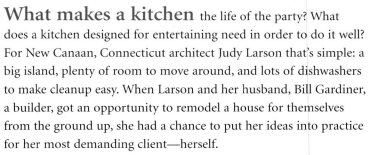

What makes a kitchen the life of the party? What does a kitchen designed for entertaining need in order to do it well? For New Canaan, Connecticut architect Judy Larson that's simple: a big island, plenty of room to move around, and lots of dishwashers to make cleanup easy. When Larson and her husband, Bill Gardiner, a builder, got an opportunity to remodel a house for themselves from the ground up, she had a chance to put her ideas into practice for her most demanding client—herself.

Larson started by giving herself plenty of space to work with: an 18 × 19 feet, 9-inch area for the kitchen. This was more than enough to hold the 8 × 10 feet island she wanted and still have room for passageways around and through the kitchen.

Besides wanting to provide a generous work surface for kitchen tasks normally done at an island, Larson saw this island as a big table in the middle of her kitchen—like a nineteenth century

The cooking center has a small commercial-style range with a closeby sink. Opposite the range, on the island, are a wok burner and a steamer, both counter-mounted and accessible to the cook simply by turning around. While the range has an oven, most of the baking and roasting are done in the ovens located in the butler's pantry. That's where the microwave is.

scullery table—big enough for several cooks and helpers, first to prepare meals for twenty or thirty people, then to serve them buffet style to her guests. As if that weren't enough, she designed a curved breakfast bar on one side of it and a built-in love seat facing a fireplace, on the other.

When not entertaining, Larson uses her island as a visual focal point in the house, with displays that catch the spirit of the changing seasons: pumpkins in the fall, festive Christmas decorations, then tulips in the spring. "You need a big island for this, especially if you're going to use it for cooking at the same time."

Larson's kitchen works in partnership with the 8 × 13 ft. walk-through butler's pantry she designed next to it. The pantry has a sink, a dish-washer, two freezer drawers, plus as much work counter space as in the kitchen itself. Here, too, she put the microwave and the wall ovens. One benefit of duplicating prep and cleanup centers in the pantry is to spread the work areas out so that people don't get in each other's way when getting things ready for a party.

Larson designed the butler's pantry with summer entertaining in mind; it joins the kitchen with a long covered porch. Cleaning up from summer parties happens here. The mess doesn't migrate to the kitchen.

Throughout the design process, cleanup was on Larson's mind. Her approach to this aspect of

The butler's pantry, **opposite page, links the kitchen to both a big summer porch, above, and the formal dining room. Plenty of counter space here means room for plating party meals and handling dirty dishes after the party. The wall ovens turn the pantry into a cooking and baking center. Placing the large sink, top and opposite page, and dishwasher next to them, localizes cleanup from both the indoor and outdoor dining areas.**

kitchen design is planned versatility. Besides wanting lots of dishwashers—there are three—she suggests having more than one cleanup sink. "Many people like to engage guests in the process—not just meal preparation, but also cleanup." More than one sink means more than one place where this can happen. Someone can clean up, keeping ahead of the mess—with the help of a guest, of course—while others continue with the food preparation.

This happens often at the twin farm sinks that form Larson's primary cleanup center. She sees these twin sinks as a very large double bowl sink—very large. Pots can soak in one sink while vegetables are washed in the other. A sink arrangement like this, she points out, is also a good place to bathe a small dog, perhaps one in each sink, if you have two.

Larson specified base cabinets, with deep drawers. She prefers drawer storage for keeping nonperishable boxed foods and finds them easier to use than cabinets with roll-out shelves, especially when equipped with self-closing hardware. Her wall cabinets are deeper than the standard 13 inches in order to accommodate large

Talk about a big island. This one has built-in seating that faces a kitchen fireplace. Larson wanted it big because she saw it as a multi-use table. When she and her husband entertain, it's where the smorgasbord goes. Wide spaces between the island and the counters make it easy for guests to move around and not feel crowded as they graze the food. When she does not use the island for parties, Larson likes to display seasonal items on it.

A sunlit octagonal breakfast room is an inviting space for family meals or a casual get-together with another couple. For those larger parties, the table is another serving station. A door leads to the covered porch, providing easy access to cool outdoor seating for people who have been through the buffet line.

platters. What about the trend away from wall cabinets? That's fine, she says, for contemporary styles or when you want a lot of windows in your kitchen. "But I think some things just store better in wall cabinets—coffee mugs, for example."

So do Larson's space-planning ideas work? One of her first parties proved that they do. She prepared a buffet supper for forty. Guests moved effortlessly around the island and the small breakfast table, helping themselves to entrees. Then it was on to the dessert bar in the butler's panty.

When it was over, both kitchen and pantry cleaned up well.

From the Designer

▶ To Your Kitchen

DISHWASHERS. Put in as many as you have space for. You'll use them all the time and won't regret it. **SINKS,** the same thing: Three are better than two. Pick ones with big, deep bowls—good for soaking large pots and small dogs. **DEEP DRAWERS** store packaged food, as well as cookware. Drawers work better than base cabinets with pull-out shelves and, if you've got kids, use self-closing hardware. **13-INCH-DEEP** wall cabinets may not be deep enough for big platters, so have them made a little deeper.

The stone fireplace, **top right,** used every day in the winter, is a focal point for the kitchen.

Twin sinks, **top left,** let the cooks keep up with cleanup chores in one bowl, while using the other one for food preparation.

A small planning desk, **right,** gives Larson a spot near the fire where she can organize her parties.

Friendly Formality

"I wanted a place to slice my bread," one of the owners said to Connecticut designer Mary Jo Peterson, CKD. It was just one of quite a few things on the list for improving a dated kitchen in a 1720s house.

It took Peterson two tries before she understood that these owners were less interested in space planning and more interested in how the new space felt. "What turned out to be important," Peterson remembers, "was the character of the kitchen, the parameters of the people using the space, not the space itself." This is not to say that making the space work efficiently wasn't important; it was. But it was complicated by a staircase that couldn't be moved. It was going to be smack in the middle of any new design Peterson drew.

The owners are great cooks. Often, they'll call friends on a Friday afternoon and ask them over to taste-test a new recipe they're

Placing the commercial-style range at a 45-degree angle breaks up a long wall that could easily look like a railroad siding. By pointing the range toward the eating table, the kitchen merges seamlessly into the eating area, effectively unifying them into one space in which people move from cooking to conversation when the meal is served.

A custom-made **furniture** piece **disguises** a stairwell that couldn't be moved

trying out. What they wanted was a friendly, open kitchen in which they could cook together with guests and then sit down together to enjoy the meal with wine and good conversation.

Peterson's plan for this called for keeping the food preparation, baking, and cooking centers on the right side of the staircase. There is a large, dual-purpose sink on this side of the kitchen, along with a dishwasher for pots and pans. On the other side of the staircase, she installed a sink and dishwasher specifically for dishes, glassware, and silver: items stored in this part of the kitchen.

This was the bones of the plan. Fleshing it out, creating the character of the kitchen was the job of cabinet maker Sam Cousins. Cousins is the late Julia Childs' nephew. He remembered the times he spent in her kitchen, a memory that taught him that kitchen design has as much to do with making the kitchen part of the lives of those who use it as it does with choosing the right appliances.

Cousins likened the big staircase to a 500-pound elephant in the kitchen that you couldn't shoo away. He suggested that the owners accentuate it; call attention to it, not as a staircase but as a piece of furniture. They agreed. Cousins dressed it with tiger maple. Depending on how you view it, it looks like it could be a walk-in pantry, or perhaps a free-standing storage and display unit. Doors leading to the stairs are false fronts designed to look like drawers below a cabinet. Continuing the furniture idea, Cousins built two tables that face into the kitchen's cooking area. The butternut cabinets, painted, sanded and painted again for a distressed look, were also handmade by Cousins.

So what about the character everyone was after—those people parameters? "Well," say the owners, "we have cocktails in the kitchen, everyone helps cook, then we sit down for an intimate dinner. After that, when we're well-fed, you fill up both dishwashers and go to bed."

That's my idea of a good party.

▶ To Your Kitchen

From the Designer

IF YOU CAN'T CHANGE something in your kitchen, think about disguising it—turn it into a visual focal point. Like turning a lemon into lemonade. **LOOK CLOSELY** at small, apparently useless spaces. You may be able to use them for display areas. **GROUP YOUR** work centers into work zones that take into account traffic flow through the kitchen. **THE RIGHT SPACE** plan is only one half of kitchen design. Accessories and decorative details make a new kitchen match your personality.

Made from the same tiger maple used to disguise the stairway, the accessory table, opposite page, adds to the idea that this kitchen is a collection of fine furniture.

A cleanup and storage area for dishes and glasses, left, is used for additional prep space and for party hors d'oeuvres. The shallow plate display shows how a tough space can be put to good use.

The large planning center, below left, sits between the cooking center and the table where casual meals are eaten.

A service bar, below right, is the cocktail center for both the kitchen and dining room. Under the poster is a formal eating area for the owners' two standard poodles.

European Vision

A white canvas for the art on the walls, the furnishings in the rooms, and the visual impact of the kitchen. This is very European—not the Americanized version of a European look, but a close replica of a Belgian manor house, or perhaps a French country house on the Mediterranean. It's exactly what the owner, a European businessman, wanted and what builder Frederick Allen and kitchen designer Julia Zemp gave him.

The kitchen is intentionally sparse to call attention to its two focal points: a French range, made by the same company that provided painter Claude Monet with one in 1908, and the radius window above the sink. It was custom-made to match the interior archways and separate the first-floor rooms.

What strikes you first in this kitchen is how white the walls are. They are white-washed plaster, the plaster hand-applied to create an imperfect, rustic finish. But unlike plaster walls in old European

A crisp white plaster wall with oak accents and accessories results in a kitchen with a simple, but eye-catching color scheme. The radius of the arch above the pass-through, which links the kitchen and dining room, was selected by trial and error. The same radius curve is used on the kitchen window and on the deep niches in the pantry.

homes, these walls have been sealed to prevent them from becoming chalky. Two other features the owner insisted on—in fact, he provided the material for them—are the hand-planed ceiling beams, imported from France, and the floor, made from 300-year-old roof tiles salvaged from French villas and refinished for use in this manner.

With these pure white walls as a backdrop, the owner wanted a kitchen that looked as though it had been there for a hundred years. Kitchen designer Zemp knew exactly what he was after. Her British background made it easy for her to visualize and design a historic European kitchen.

"I was given a U-shape layout by the architect, and the owner had picked the French range and decided on the other appliances. My job was so much in space planning, as to give this kitchen more visual interest by using level changes and moving the eye back and forth by using niches in the walls."

There are no base cabinets as Americans think of them. Instead, quarter-sawn drawers are fitted into the white plaster walls. The sink cabinet is more like a piece of old oak furniture. Zemp had it built 2 inches higher than the surrounding countertops, specifically to set it apart and make it look like an antique slid into a spot that had been left open for it.

A small kitchen table the owner imported from France is the kitchen's centerpiece—literally. Placed almost dead center, it becomes the element that unifies the legs of the U-shape kitchen. It adds to the European manor house feel the owner wanted, and, of course, it's a functional work surface.

Open niches, white-washed plaster walls, and natural oak are elements of true European design

From the Designer

▶ To Your Kitchen

ANTIQUES ADD a lot to a kitchen, so don't be afraid to use them—not just small things you display, but larger items like tables, that you use. **SMALL SPACES,** especially if they are in corners, too often are relegated to open tray storage. Try something different, a built-in that's both functional and looks good.

The dining room, **above left, is connected to the kitchen by a pass-through.**

Both appealing to the eye and an innovative use of a small space, the custom-made storage space built into a base cabinet, above right, holds two trays that are ready to use. These trays were also custom-made to fit the spaces where they would be stored.

While not exactly a full-fledged planning center, this phone and message alcove, left, built into the pantry, is a convenient place to keep track of lists.

There are no wall cabinets either. Zemp remembers her client saying to her that he didn't want any because, "all you do is store rubbish in them. If you have them, you accumulate more rubbish." There are, however, three open shelves, there to provide a visual break from the white walls as much to give the owner a place to display some old pottery.

Some of what might be kept in wall cabinets is stored on open shelves on the refrigerator wall and niches above it. These shelves were Zemp's idea. To the left of the refrigerator—itself disguised as an armoire—Zemp took a foot of space that could easily have been left blank and made shelves. Her mixing of oak and plaster repeats the motif used elsewhere in the kitchen. In the pantry, the deep niches are possible because the walls are thicker than normal. Niches in the pantry, these with the same radius arch of the kitchen window, are high enough for tall books and deep enough for small appliances.

The French-made range, above left, is finished in white to be consistent with the kitchen's color scheme. Behind it, Zemp chose white tile to match the statuary marble countertops.

Attached to the side of the kitchen table is a brass rail, above right, with hooks from which towels and other items can hang in a ready-to-use location.

In Good Company

Halloween is Ellen Dickson's favorite holiday and favorite reason to have a party. A Chicago architect, she's spent years designing kitchens for others while leaving her own kitchen "as is." When the ongoing remodeling of her 1940s-era house got around to the kitchen, she had the opportunity to try the ideas her clients had rejected as a bit too far out.

Dickson's kitchen isn't large, nor is the dining room that opens onto it. Adding space to either room wasn't in the plans, so it was a question of rearranging the space she had to make it more efficient for herself, for her family, and for the parties that regularly fill up her kitchen with friends. In her mind, too, Dickson wanted a kitchen that, well, didn't exactly look like a kitchen.

What does a non-kitchen kitchen look like? No wall cabinets for starters. Dickson specifically wanted something other than what she calls the boom, boom, boom of a row of wall cabinets staring

The kitchen hutch, sometimes with Nikkita the cat holding court, is the first thing people see when they enter the kitchen. Dickson designed it as a piece of furniture whose lower doors recall turn-of-the-twentieth-century pie safes. The stained glass window was bought in England; Dickson attributes its perfect fit in the window to plain good luck.

A small **kitchen** feels **larger** if it has no wall cabinets

out at you. So her new kitchen doesn't have any. The immediate result is that the room feels bigger and is less claustrophobic.

But about storage—all the stuff that every kitchen has? It has to go somewhere. Pantries are one alternative, and Dickson set out to design one that was interesting and stored a lot. "However, I don't like full-depth pantries. They're too solid and too imposing." This led her to try an idea she'd been suggesting to clients without much success—a dovecote storage wall.

The dovecote she designed takes up the entire wall to the left of the refrigerator. It has nine storage cubbies with doors mounted on hardware that lets them flip up and hide inside the cubby. "We had enough counter space to do what we wanted," Dickson said. "But in a pinch, doors on the lower cubbies can be flipped up to give us more." The granite counters run under them.

Dickson's second alternative to wall cabinets is a large hutch she designed to look like a piece of furniture. She built it around an existing window and placed it so that guests coming in the front door look directly at it—their first impression of the kitchen. The hutch separates the kitchen and dining room; Dickson uses it to store items used in both rooms.

The island is the heart of this kitchen. Dickson kept the prep sink small because she wanted as much counter area as possible. This is where she puts the party appetizers and where people sit—on the stools until they are all taken, then on the island. Party guests also sit on the counters running along the kitchen's perimeter. Another advantage of no wall cabinets.

A storage wall, in the form of a dovecote, substitutes for wall cabinets, which Dickson didn't want. Doors to the cubbies lift up and slide back out of the way. The door design repeats the pie-safe motif used in the hutch.

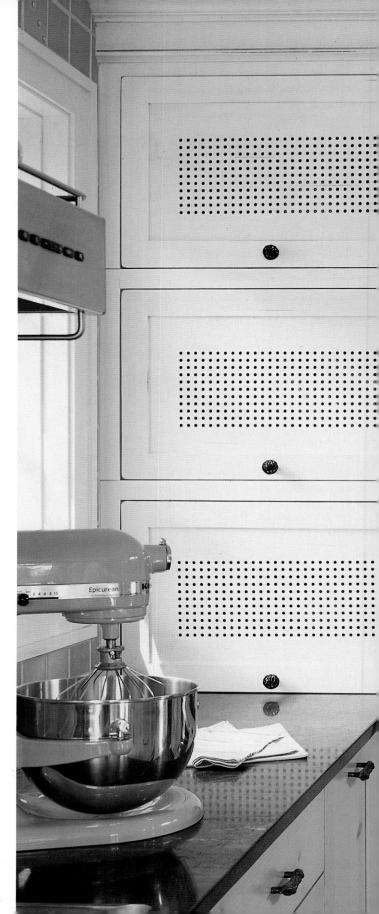

From the Designer

▶ To Your Kitchen

GO WITH THINGS that catch your eye. Don't be afraid to mix styles. **LOOK FOR ALTERNATIVES** to wall cabinets—a hutch or some other piece of furniture that can be used for storage. **DON'T AVOID COLOR.** Real estate agents like white because it's not risky at resale time. But they don't have to live in your kitchen, you do. **CREATE KITCHEN FOCAL POINTS** with color changes, appliance placements, or art work and displays. **DON'T BE AFRAID** to make a mistake. You can fix it in a few years.

The island, left, is the kitchen's primary food preparation center, with the prep sink close to both the storage wall and the refrigerator. The oven in the island is a "quick cook" unit designed to cook food that shouldn't be microwaved,

A big collector of folk art, Dickson put a hand-made sequined crow and rabbit, top right, on the counter where she can enjoy them.

A colorful kitchen was also on Dickson's mind. "I wanted to play with colors people might not be familiar with. For me they are happy colors." This led her to a butternut squash finish for the cabinets, which play off of yellow subway tiles for the kitchen walls. The blue walls in the dining room contrast with these happy colors, with the white hutch acting as a transition element between the rooms.

Then there's the art—the plates on the range hood and the sequined rabbit and crow in the corner near the sink, plus the prints in the dining room. There's just enough so the people enjoying a party in these rooms get the point that life is fun.

The dining room **doubles as another buffet for parties starting in the kitchen and moving through the dining room to the backyard patio. The lights over the table are '50s retro; the prints date from the '40s and were made by the same company that made posters for the Grand Ole Opry in Nashville.**

Bay Area Beckons

Saturday morning in the hills above Berkeley, California. Mark Kendall stands at his 60-inch, custom-made cooktop and griddle, ready for some short-order cooking as his kids and their sleepover friends wander in for a hearty breakfast, including fresh eggs from chickens raised by the Kendalls in their backyard. Well, that's one way to entertain, so is a pasta party for one hundred hungry teenagers. However Mark Kendall and his wife Jane entertain, they knew they needed a big kitchen to do what they wanted.

As a builder and developer, Kendall had the structural knowledge to understand what was possible when he decided to remodel his house to get that kitchen. What he chose was to clear span a large, open space with a vaulted ceiling, and then top that ceiling with a seven-sided skylight mounted in a cupola. "Unique" is an overused word when it comes to writing about remodeling and

A full-service bar is the centerpiece of this kitchen, which comes alive when family and friends arrive for food and fun. From his spot inside the bar, Mark Kendall—literally in the center of things—gets the party going while his wife Jane prepares the meal in the work trench running along two of the island's closed sides.

interior design, but this skylight truly is. What makes it work is a steel compression ring and the steel beams that radiate from it. No posts or cross bracing are needed. Jane Kendall remembers holding her breath when it went in. Steel, of course, is not exactly eye-catching. To fix this, Kendall found old railroad ties that he affixed to the steel beams. The result is a ceiling that looks like its support comes from heavy pieces of hewn lumber.

Arsenio Perez Jr., CKD, from KB Associates in San Mateo, California, helped Jane Kendall work out an efficient kitchen to put under the cupola. Actually, Perez helped both Kendalls since they wanted different and potentially contradictory features in this kitchen.

Mark Kendall wanted not just a wetbar, he wanted something approaching a real bar. "For us, this kitchen was to be a place where we could spend most of our time," he said, "a place to entertain in a convivial private bar atmosphere with the kitchen right next to it."

Jane Kendall wanted to cook.

Perez devised a plan that worked for both of them. The island, in the shape of a hollow square, has plenty of room for Kendall to bartend. And everything a well-equipped bar needs is there: small sink, a pure water dispenser, a cooler for wine, beer and soda, and plenty of cabinets for glassware and accessories.

Positioned directly under the cupola with its seven-sided skylight, the bar and the kitchen get natural light at any time of day. The bar's raised wood serving counter was matched with the height of the bar stools for the comfort of the guests. On the bar's other side, the granite counters are a standard height for easy food preparation.

For Jane's part of the kitchen—the cooking part—Perez laid out an L-shaped work trench that lets her move easily from the major centers built in both sides of it. He put the refrigerator, the freezer, and two refrigerator drawers for fresh produce near the inside corner of the L. Across from this, on the outside corner, he put the prep sink, which is where Jane normally works when the couple entertains. Its corner location lets Jane talk with guests sitting at the island.

There is also a pantry at the apex of the L, which together with the refrigerators and freezer, forms the kitchen's centralized storage center. The pantry almost wasn't there. That corner space had been a hallway leading to the kids' bedrooms. "Hey wait a minute," Jane Kendall recalls saying. "What I don't need is for kids to be funneled directly into the part of the kitchen where I work." And she did need a pantry. So the plan was changed and the hallway got a new life in the redraw.

Jane Kendall is left-handed. Perez took this into account in placing appliances. As it happens, the configuration of the 60-inch cooktop comes with the bank of four burners on the left side. The left-hand position of the pot filler makes this setup even more convenient. For the baking center, Perez placed the wall ovens as far to the right as possible so that he could give Jane a set-down area to the left of them. One of the dishwashers, a drawer model, is at the left of the cleanup sink. Jane uses this one. But two other

The L-shaped work trench **gives Jane Kendall the room she needs to move between her cleanup sink and the cooktop. The island prep sink at the corner of the L is just a few steps away from the pantry and the refrigerator.**

Refrigeration, including two drawers, right, is centralized on the wall directly behind the prep sink.

A large farm sink, opposite page, handles cleanup chores. To the left of it is a dishwasher drawer, put in that position because Jane Kendall is left-handed.

The open plate rack, below left, is for everyday dishes—dishes whose bright yellow pattern fits with the kitchen color scheme established by the tile work.

Diamond-shaped tiles, below right, in four bright colors, create a mosaic backsplash behind the cooktop. The pot filler, mounted above the left bank of burners, is another convenience for southpaws.

dishwashers are placed to the right of the sink—her kids are right-handed and she wanted to make it easy for them to do the dishes. An idea worth remembering.

Besides the bar, what grabs your eye as you walk into this kitchen is the tile work at the cooktop. Jane wanted some kind of an eye-catching tile design for the backsplash and hood, but couldn't decide on a color. So she picked them all—four bright impact colors on diamond-shaped tiles for decorative accents on the cooktop backsplash and the range hood. Her husband calls these colors a California Tuscany blend. Playful. The same blend of bright colors, this time in square tiles, forms the backsplash under the open plate rack on the opposite side of the kitchen.

The chase, hiding the hood and duct work, is pure yellow and runs to the ceiling. But this big yellow "chimney" also has the effect of lowering the perception of ceiling height which, as Mark says, helps bring the ceiling details down to eye level. Another trick Mark used to cut the perceived distance between the ceiling and counters was to install taller wall cabinets and then to use the space on top of them to display big items such as large platters and baskets. The big clock above the sink also scales back the space.

▶ To Your Kitchen

From the Designer

LEFT-HANDED? Then make sure to tell your designer that you want countertop layouts that favor your left side, like left-oriented setdown areas next to the cooktop and range, and dishwashers placed to the left of the sink. **ISLANDS ARE CONVERSATIONAL MAGNETS.** If you entertain regularly and have the space, think about an island large enough to accommodate stools to make it easy for guests to hang out. **DON'T BE AFRAID** of bright colors. They can add interest to your kitchen and help unify big spaces.

5

Kitchens for Cooks

Ah, cooking. A tasty way to relax for many of us. In the 21st century, new appliances will open up limitless possibilities, and new kitchens will be designed to increase the joy of cooking for one cook or several.

Food with a View

Call this a dream kitchen for a stay-at-home, telecommuting couple and their two children. It's used at least three times a day for meals, plus countless excursions for snacks. In the evening it becomes the center for entertaining and, at all times, the kitchen windows framing views of the Arizona mountains above Tucson make it an inviting place to be.

Kathy and Larry, both home-office professionals wanted a relaxed kitchen large enough for everyone—family, friends, and guests—to be there when Kathy cooks. Kathy's background as a professional caterer influenced both her choice of appliances and the layout she wanted for them. "My desire was to create different centers in my kitchen, including a baking center near my ovens and warming drawers, plus a surface cooking area with easy access to all my cooking tools, spices and refrigerator drawers." Kathy also wanted two sinks—one, near the cooktop, for washing food about

The working part of this kitchen has two prep centers, each with a sink, two cooking centers—one at the big cooktop; the other at the smaller cook sink—and two dishwashers. The open spindle to the left of the cooktop (also shown above) is called a "chef's accessory tree." Kathy uses it for utensils and condiments. It's handy when there aren't nearby wall cabinets.

Shallow Box **beams** create a
coffered-ceiling look and
minimize the effect of the
deep, structural **ceiling** supports

to be prepared and the other for washing dishes and general cleanup. She also had definite ideas about the appliance brands she wanted and how she wanted the traffic to flow through and around the kitchen. Finally, since this was a remodel, both Kathy and Frank wanted a view of the mountains that they'd been waiting ten years to see.

Some wish list for Elizabeth Spengler of Dorado Kitchens in Tucson. It was complicated, too, because finding room for everything Kathy and Larry wanted meant expanding out to incorporate a porch that would provide the space needed for the new kitchen. Doing this meant Spengler had to work out an artistic solution of a major structural problem. And with all those new windows, there wasn't going to be a lot of room for wall cabinets.

Spengler's solution was a plan based on a long peninsula and a big island. Together they gave Kathy the countertop work space she wanted. And at more than double the normal depth, Spengler could build in base cabinet storage drawers on both sides. The island includes a raised glass top used both for eating and for preparation of pastries and hot hors d'oeurvres cooked in the twin wall ovens behind it, and for plating when the food comes out. Following Kathy's wish, Spengler put a warming drawer under each oven. This reflects Kathy's catering experience.

Structurally, the big open room required support beams held up by posts. To disguise this requirement, Spengler designed open stainless steel shelf supports at the end of the peninsula. One of the vertical supports holds up the ceiling beam, the other is purely decorative. On the ceiling, too, smaller non-structural box beams set at right angles to those providing support, create a pattern that looks planned rather than required.

▶ To Your Kitchen

From the Designer

APPLIANCES are you own personal choice. If you know what you want, don't let your designer talk you out of them. **IF YOU NEED** support columns, think of them as potential design elements that can enhance the look of your kitchen. **USE THE SAME TRICK** with required ceiling beams by adding decorative box beams to create an interesting ceiling pattern. **CREATE MORE STORAGE** with wider islands and peninsulas that accommodate drawers or cabinets on both sides. This is particularly useful if your new kitchen has few or no wall cabinets. **A CORNER SINK** is a good way to get more efficient countertop work space and, if you have views, it won't block them.

The round, custom-made hood, top left page, provides the needed exhaust capacity for the high-heat cooking Kathy likes to do. It is also a room divider that doesn't obstruct the great mountain views.

Twin-bowl corner sinks, above right, give two cooks, working at adjacent counters, access to water without getting in each other's way. The high-rise commercial faucet makes it easy to clean pots too large for dishwashers.

More than a planning center, Kathy's computer station, left, on the other side of the peninsula, also doubles as an auxiliary office for her professional work.

American Nostalgia

All these wonderful things; these wonderful memories. Americana. The pretzel dispensers, the old jar for soda straws— remember those?—a sink and counter that onced graced an 1890s candy store. Can a 21st century kitchen also be a scrapbook? Of course it can. This kitchen, whose feel on first glance, was ahead of its time for 1910, is right up to date for our new century.

This is Ann's kitchen. Ann is a native of Ohio with a lifelong love of rustic Midwestern antiques. Now living with her husband in the Chicago area, she had remodeled her kitchen over a decade earlier to give it the farmhouse-feel she wanted. Two things pushed her to remodel again: The first was her husband's desire to add a small wine cooler; the second was when Ann attended a demonstration for the Aga Cooker at the Insignia Kitchens and Baths Design Group in Barrington, Illinois. A word about this appliance is in order here. It's British-made, runs on gas, is always

Kitchens are more than just places to cook. They are reflections of your personality. This comes across through the things in your kitchen that are important to you. A collector for many years, Ann wanted a kitchen with no visual seams to separate the work centers from the display areas. EAT. Well that's what a kitchen helps you do, so why not say so?

on, and has no temperature controls. Four ovens maintain four different, pre-set temperatures that are supposed to meet most baking requirements. On top there are two large hot plates, one for boiling, the other for simmering. A different way of cooking and not that common in America, but for Ann, who has had her recipes published, it was the way she wanted to cook once she discovered she could.

This is a big range. Finding space for it in a new kitchen was the problem faced by Susan Waters, Ann's kitchen designer, who at the time of this project was working for Insignia. That space was found when Ann agreed to give up her dining room. But this led to another problem: with the walls down, the enlarged room was long and narrow and could easily end up looking like two kitchens widely separated from each other. Unifying this space was Waters' number one task.

She did it with an island in the shape of a T with a curved top that she placed in the center of the new room. Ann didn't want to alter the older part of her kitchen, either by moving her cleanup center or by replacing a hundred-year-old copper sink that anchored it, so Waters put a prep sink in the island accesible to both the range and the refrigerator. The island also got the most modern of conveniences, a soda gun mounted over a trough sink that's mostly used as an ice bucket.

Over a hundred years old, the hand-pounded copper sink, built into a display cabinet of the same age, is still the one Ann uses every day for cleanup chores. It's in the older part of the kitchen that Susan Waters integrated it into the new design.

The small range, in the background, is a second cooking center. Next to it, an etagère holds a collection of pots and pans hand-made by Ohio artist Don Drum. These aren't just pretty accessories; Ann uses them every day.

Houses are made of bricks & beams
Homes are made of love & dreams

The wine-red and light birch color scheme for the cabinets harks back to old, comfortable farm kitchens, which is what Ann wanted. It creates an inviting backround for the antiques and memorabilia she has collected over the years and that she wants to see every day as she works in her kitchen.

Color fashion changes over the decades, and Waters was lucky to find a small cabinet shop that perfectly matched the wine-red and light oak on the cabinets in the older part of the kitchen. She was luckier still to find a batch of the same brick Ann used for countertops thirteen years ago, so the new ones matched.

During the remodeling, Ann bought an antique hutch. There was no good place for it in Waters' plan, so it went on a far wall where it partially blocked two windows—another eclectic touch.

Remember the wine cooler that Ann's husband wanted? Well Ann and Waters almost didn't fit it in. It was the last thing added, completing the wish list for this kitchen, which spans two centuries.

▶ To Your Kitchen

From the Designer

GLASS HALF-FRONT DRAWER fronts create an old-fashioned look without compromising storage space in the drawers behind them. **LOOKING FOR ANTIQUE PIECES?** Make sure they fit the space you have in mind. Talk with your designer before you buy anything. **CABINET COMPANIES** don't just sell cabinets. Ask them about distressed finishes, if you want this look.

The four-oven Aga Cooker, **top**, is a traditional English stove designed in the 1920s and little changed since. It's the kitchen's functional focal point and perfectly defines the term "cooking center."

The other kitchen focal point is the island, combining an eclectic mix of styles: wainscotting from the early twentieth century, soda fountain stools right out of the 1950s, and the monorail lighting system above it that couldn't be more "today."

Cordon Bleu

Stand and spin. That's what a chef does when she works in the kitchen of her own restaurant. The idea is to stand in one place that allows you to move effortlessly from the prepping station to the cooking station. If you're that chef, trained at the Cordon Bleu in Paris and have spent years cooking for customers in your own restaurant, when you cook at home for your family and for guests, you want to stand and spin.

Julie Young, CKD, of Carmel Kitchens, on California's Monterey Peninsula, put herself through design school working in a restaurant kitchen; her first job was designing restaurant kitchens. So when a Cordon Bleu-trained client asked Young to design the kitchen in her home, Young had a good idea of what she wanted. "It's the cooking line," says Young, "prep and cooking areas right next to each other on the same counter: a linear work flow. To do this right you have to throw any idea about triangles out the window."

More than an efficient **working environment for a professional chef, this kitchen has a snack center for the kids next to the prepping and cooking area. A cooler for milk and juice is within easy reach of the banquet where the kids do their homework and play games. The kid-friendly microwave is mounted halfway up from the floor. It's too low for easy adult use.**

The narrow, 11-foot-wide space Young had to work with after her clients remodeled their house was an advantage. A stand-and-spin arrangement was all that the space could handle. This is why the cooktop is so close to the sink. If you recall those kitchen efficiency tests conducted by Steidl back in the late 1940s, that we discussed in Chapter 1, it's clear that this arrangement is a very efficient one. Steidl had noted that when a cook is at the sink, she likes to stay there, looking over at what's cooking on the range by just turning her head. Exactly what happens here.

Not surprisingly, Young's client knew which appliances she wanted—all bought for function. There's no warming drawer because she plates and serves her guests, seated around the island, right from the cooktop. There's only one sink, not by choice, but because in this part of California there are water-use restrictions and only one was allowed.

At 3 × 8 ft., the island isn't large—there wasn't space for anything bigger—but its size and location define a galley kitchen, one of the most efficient working layouts you can have. The island adds additional counter workspace, provides a seating area, and acts as a barrier between the cooking zone and the entertaining zone. What do we mean by zones?

Young's design combined the principles of work center space-planning, her client's desire for efficient, restaurant food-line cooking, and Young's idea to create activity zones.

Preparation and cooking are done between the sink and the cooktop. Plating of just-cooked food happens on the counter to the left of the cooktop. Young designed the island with a knee hole on the cooking side. A service cart hides in the hole, coming out when needed. After serving her guests, the chef pulls up a chair and sits down there to join them.

The beverage zone, right, is on the other side of the island. While the chef cooks and serves guests seated at the island, her husband handles the wine and then the coffee. Glasses and cups are kept in the built-in buffet.

The snack center setup, opposite page, is completely kid-oriented. The cooler door opens toward where they sit, not toward people in the kitchen, and a deep drawer for snacks means that the kids can get what they want without bothering Mom, the chef.

Stairs at the back of the kitchen, below right, lead to a deck used for outdoor eating. Both were added as part of the remodeling.

From the Designer

▶ To Your Kitchen

24-INCH-DEEP BACKSPLASHES offer more flexibility than the standard 18-inch height because they can accommodate bigger countertop appliances. **ONE SINGLE BOWL** sink is better than a double bowl if you can only have one sink. The big bowl can handle all different sizes of pots and pans, and is more versatile when you wash produce. **WANT A COFFEE MACHINE** in your kitchen? If space is cramped, add a pull-out shelf built into the counter to give yourself a place to keep the cups you'll be using. **OTTOMANS** in front of banquette seating are a flexible alternative to coffee tables; they are easily moved around, are places for food trays, and can provide additional seating.

Zone one is the cooking zone—a classic food line. Working from right to left, the cook preps at the sink, cooks on the range, and plates at the counter to the left of the range. Little movement is needed until it's time to plate the food.

Zone two is what Young calls the beverage zone. "This is a kitchen for gourmet dinners with small groups of friends," says Young, who has been to some of them. "Wine—this is California, remember—is part of entertaining. So where is the wine going to be and how do we get to it quickly?" With the cook at her food line, her husband serves the wine from the other side of the island. Glasses and wine are kept in the built-in glass-door buffet. There's plenty of room for him to move around the island without crowding the seated guests. After dinner, he does the same thing with the coffee, pulling lattés from the restaurant espresso machine hooked up to a water line at its own work center. When chilled desserts are on the menu, he can get them from the refrigerator without coming into the food prep and cooking zone.

Zone three is for the kids—most of the time. It's a combination work, play, and snack center in the kitchen but outside the food line—what we've also called the "trench." The under-counter cooler holds milk and juice, and the door swing is for the convenience of the kids, not the cook. For parties, the snack center provides casual seating for guests. The ottomans double as coffee tables that can be moved to where they are needed.

The kitchen got its red and gold color scheme from the owners' fondness for the colors of Washington-state Rainier cherries: red and gold. The red cork floor came first, followed by the built-in buffet which, by chance, offered cherry-red as a standard color.

Inspired Amateurs

The Clarks, not their real name, knew they had a problem. Their high-priced kitchen designer had just told them that they couldn't take down the wall separating their about-to-be remodeled kitchen and the existing greenhouse. Goodbye to an airy open plan. Goodbye to all that natural light and the great views of the lake they lived on. Why? The feng shui, said the designer, would be wrong. Positive kitchen energy would escape out of the greenhouse windows.

The Clarks looked at each other and decided by silent body language that they could design this kitchen themselves. Fifteen minutes later it was goodbye to the designer. She wasn't the first.

There wasn't much space to work with, and the size of the old kitchen stayed about the same. Even with the greenhouse now part of the kitchen, they were limited to a smallish island that could still be used as a buffet for casual entertaining.

The island is designed so that both husband and wife can work at it—across from each other. Mr. Clark prefers to work seated, so the trough sink is within his easy reach. While doing his prep work he can slide the chopping waste to an in-counter receptacle. Drawers on this side of the island store a duplicate set of knives and other food preparation utensils.

Daylight from the greenhouse makes the open kitchen shine

The cleanup side of the island, opposite page, has two dishwashers—both with adjustable shelves to accommodate large pots. Besides pre-dishwasher cleanup, the sink between them serves the prep needs of the cook. Food prep for meals destined for the wall ovens happens on the other side of the island.

A custom-made cabinet at the end of the island, above, creates storage in what could have been a wasted area. With its overly deep shelves, this space is reserved for large serving trays, which the Clarks regularly use when they entertain.

Most important, the Clarks wanted a kitchen where they both could cook, at the same time, without getting in each other's way and without fighting over who gets to chop with the chef's knife. The best arrangement they could think of was to work across from each other over a shared island with duplicated features needed to cook simultaneously. Two sinks went in—a big one for her and a smaller trough sink for him. So did two knife and utensil drawers and two receptacles for food waste.

The Clarks didn't work alone. The architect who had done an earlier addition was brought in to deal with technical issues and figure out the best way to disguise a support post required to hold up the ceiling after another wall came down. (Stainless steel cladding was used to match the counter on either side of the cooktop.)

The Clarks knew some excellent local custom-cabinet companies and refused to spend more money than they needed for cabinets that offered less than what they wanted. They picked Ken Heise from the Wood Shop of Avon in Minneapolis, to design the cabinets and help with the space planning. This, after they rejected the second kitchen designer, who insisted that only German cabinets could be used.

The locally made cabinets are excellent and Heise's attention to detail ensured that the Clarks got every inch of possible storage in the island and in a corner cabinet, where he installed a two-tiered lazy Susan.

The Clarks were told they should get rid of their old wood floor. Nonsense. They patched it where walls were removed and then had it sanded and refinished.

For the causal dining area in the greenhouse—used all the time for parties—the Clarks bought a glass table and put contemporary, see-through chairs around it. The light green-tinted glass table was the starting point for the translucent green glass backsplash behind the cooktop—an alternative they preferred to a tile backsplash and a color they preferred to white. No grout lines to worry about, either.

Under the table, a canvas oil-cloth art rug adds a strong touch of color. Done by Minnesota artist Mark Larson, it interprets the works of Howard Hotchkin, the Clarks' favorite artist. The rug, table, and greenhouse make Mr. Clark the happiest. Sitting at it in the summer, with greenhouse doors open, he watches the feng shui fly away. The moral here: Stand up for what you want. Designers can help you but if they don't, remember it's your kitchen. At the end of the day, the designer gets to go home; you have to stay and live with whatever was done or not done.

Cold water spigots over the cooktop or range are popular 21st century accessories. They let you fill pots where they are used or add water while cooking. New, shallow cooktops allow utensil drawers to be placed under them. The translucent green backsplash was created by painting the wall a shade of light green and then placing a sheet of clear glass over it. The same glass, but this time sanded, was used for the door fronts on the cabinets flanking the cooktop.

A canvas oil-cloth art rug, under the glass table, left, adds a bright color accent to a room dominated by shades of green and light brown.

Planning centers are an important element in 21st century kitchens. Below left, we see a small desk in the greenhouse, placed where it can get plenty of natural light, yet not far from the island.

The positioning of the cleanup and prep sinks, below right, reflects the way both cooks like to work—face-to-face on either side of the island. The trough sink, when not used for prep, doubles as a wine bucket at parties.

147

Finders Keepers

This is a kitchen with views. There are outside ones of New York's Hudson River valley and inside ones of the found objects the owners have collected over the years. Not just collectors, these owners are also excellent cooks, which presented Carrie Deane Corcoran of Kitchens by Deane in Stamford, Connecticut with the challenge of designing a kitchen that was a perfect match of efficiency and personality.

Deane Corcoran remembers walking into the old kitchen: It was long and narrow, with not much visible through the windows. Nor was it easy to move around or through it. She also recalls the owners telling her that they wanted to interact with their guests as they prepared meals. But they didn't want guests to see the mess that normally results from cooking a complex meal.

The kitchen's functional center is its long island. In it Deane Corcoran mounted surface cooking units to handle every possible

The 8-foot-long custom range hood provides ventilation for four burners, a wok burner, a deep fryer, and a grill. A high-capacity blower motor provides the exhaust power to vent cooking heat when all those appliances are used simultaneously. The blower is mounted on the roof in order to lessen the fan noise in the kitchen.

cooking task: four standard gas burners, a wok burner, a deep fryer, and a grill. Using any of them, the cook, or both cooks, face into the adjoining room. A raised bar on the island is a convenient place for guests to taste what's being cooked or to just chat with the cooks as they work. It also visually separates the kitchen from the dining room.

Deane Corcoran put two big sinks for cleanup in the counter directly behind all those surface cooking units, creating an efficient galley arrangement similar to a stand-and-spin setup. Two dishwasher drawers to the right of these sinks handle whatever the restaurant high-rise rinser faucet can't. The smaller prep sink, she put in the island close to the refrigerator and the pantry. In this location, it's accessible from the adjoining room without entering into the work trench.

Now, Deane Corcoran had to find places for all those old objects the owners wanted on display in their new kitchen. The first was a collection of glass jars, actually used for holding staples. Deane Corcoran designed an eight-shelf display unit for them to the left of double built-in ovens. It's handy to the prep sink and the counter area between the sink and the surface cooking units—the kitchen's food preparation center.

The next found object was an old screen door from a bakery touting its very good bread. The owners bought it years ago and wanted to use it. Deane Corcoran fashioned it as a sliding door to cover the pantry shelves. Well, not exactly. It only

The big island, finished in rustic pine, was designed with a prep sink on the left and a small planning desk on the right. The island's raised back hides the cooking appliances from people in the dining room.

▶ To Your Kitchen

USING FOUND OBJECTS in your kitchen can create surprise; they can bring out your personality. But don't force them into a space. It will lead to something that looks like a mistake. **DON'T BE AFRAID** to take down a wall to get the views you want or to improve trafffic flow. **A RAISED BACK** on an island hides cooking appliances, so your guests see you, not the mess.

Good cooks like fast cleanup. That's easy with the commercial, high-rise rinser faucet, top left.

Showing off the owners' personality is an important part of this kitchen's design, which includes open shelving, top right, for their jar collection.

Two steps lead to the lower part of the kitchen, left. Deane Corcoran put a third sink there to handle cooking done on the deck and for potting plants.

covers one side of the pantry shelving; the other side is always open, though it slides back and forth so the owners can decide which side of the pantry they want to close off.

On the other side of the kitchen, opposite this sliding door, is a large 1920s-era Italian olive oil poster. Making sure there was wall space to hang it was something Deane Corcoran had to consider. Fortunately, the owners didn't need the storage space.

As a warm, inviting backdrop for these found objects, Deane Corcoran selected pine cabinets with a light honey finish. And for island facing, she chose knotty pine boards.

Refrigeration in this kitchen is split between a 36-inch refrigerator/freezer built into a wall and two refrigerator drawers mounted underneath the food prep counter. The drawers keep meats and produce close to where they will be cleaned and cooked. The pantry, with its single, antique sliding door, is in the background.

6

Living Kitchens

In the 21st century, the kitchen will be the center of everything. The rooms around it will be places to eat, play, watch TV, and relax with friends. These rooms will be open and together they will create the 21st century living room.

A Danish Vacation

Open spaces will be the rule in the 21st century; kitchens will merge seamlessly into informal eating areas and comfortable family rooms. There will be a more casual approach to family life, and many people will see their house as a vacation home they live in year-round. Living—good living—will be a key word and the motivation for a more relaxed approach to space planning and design. What we are calling the "living kitchen" will become the centerpiece of a large, open space that will be the true "living room" of the 21st century.

Windy Ridge I, a spec house in suburban Minneapolis, tests these design ideas. The open plan was developer Mark Finholt's vision, executed by architect Todd Hansen and interior designer Dawn Terizzi. Finholt saw his ideal buyer as a well-travelled, well-educated couple with preteen children—a family that would appreciate the "loft living" urban simplicity of Hanson's wide open

The kitchen is the focus of a minimalist open plan combining living, dining, and cooking spaces—three rooms that function as one—where family activities take place casually. The island, also used as breakfast bar, links the kitchen to the rest of the space. Behind the island, open shelves set against tile borrow an idea from contemporary restaurant design.

plan in which it's hard to tell where the kitchen ends and the rest of the space begins.

Finholt and his designers gave this open area a clean, Scandinavian look; they wanted the space to make the design statement, rather than have it made by the stuff in it. Wood plays an important part in this, from the warm Jara floors running throughout to the plain drawer and door style on the fir cabinets. Since wood, even light wood, has the potential to look gloomy in low light, Finholt had Hanson design a monitor window on the roof and extend it over the kitchen and dining rooms. Somewhat like the roof windows in early twentieth-century factories, monitor windows capture sunlight and let it flood into the rooms below. It gives Windy Ridge I a bright, airy feeling all day long, even in overcast weather. It also makes light an important design element for the open plan, which Terizzi took into account in developing her clutter-free interior designs.

There is a family room (just visible through the far doorway in the photo on the previous page), but Finholt chose to orient the kitchen toward the dining and living rooms. These rooms, though modern in style, are intended for the more traditional uses we remember. Sit-down dinners were in the back of everyone's mind as the plans were being drawn. So was casual conversation around the fireplace. Orienting the island so the cook looks in this direction ensures that he or she is involved with the guests at the table or in the living room.

▶ To Your Kitchen

From the Designer

IF THE ISLAND IS PART of the living space, plan it so that it fits with the surrounding design elements. Remember, you'll see the island from other rooms. **MAKE SURE** that rooms within an open space are defined by function so they still feel like separate rooms. Furniture groupings are a good way to do this. **IF YOU LIKE A MINIMAL** style, keep in mind that with a simpler, no-clutter look, any design mistakes will appear more obvious. **HARMONIZE WOOD** colors. Cabinets, trim work, and tables should complement exterior views.

A light monitor, opposite page, lets in natural light all day long. In the evening, low-voltage pendant lights, far left, hung from "hot" cables light the table.

Even in simple, minimalist designs, display space, left, is important, so cabinets on either side of the island have a recessed shelf. This also creates a striking reveal in what otherwise would have been solid wood fronts.

A storage wall of full-height cabinets, below left and right, hides the refrigerator/freezer, a closet, and a walk-in pantry.

The small planning center at the right of the pantry wall, below right, has a place for the phone, a laptop, and the alarm-system monitor.

Light and White

Open to the rooms around it, with three big work islands, this is just what a living kitchen in the 21st century should be. The surprise is that it was designed in 1992. Definitely a kitchen ahead of its time, thanks largely to architect Nina Cuccio Peck's clairvoyance.

Kitchens like this were not common, even in the late twentieth century. Open on one side to a large family room? Yes, you see that often. But a large, centrally positioned kitchen open on either side to rooms served by the kitchen was something else. Back then, an "open kitchen" had a wall. The range would back into it. This might have been the case here, too, since Peck's clients, Sally and Peter McGowan had thought seriously about buying a newly popular commercial-style range. But to accommodate that range would have required walling off either the front or the back of the kitchen to provide "backing" for it. And that would have meant blocking off

A wood island, with its cooktop and two ovens, provides a warm contrast to the white cabinets and marble counters. The cooking center in this island is across from the cleanup sink. This establishes the cook's work trench—away from the kitchen's traffic corridors. A secondary food prep area, with countertop appliances, is just beyond this trench.

The **wood** cooking center **island**, sits between two others with **easy passage** on all sides

half the natural light streaming into the kitchen all day long, light that Sally wanted.

Sally also wanted to cook from a central location in the kitchen. The answer to both her wishes was a large island that Peck designed as the cooking center. Done in wood with ornate door pulls, corbels, and carved pilasters, it's where Peck put the cooktop and two built-in ovens. Stand at this island to cook and you're right in the center of things, with a clear view of a small, casual sitting room, where family and guests can watch TV and enjoy a drink before dinner—and still talk with Sally as she cooks. If it's just the family, four stools pull up to the island so it can be used as a breakfast, lunch, or dinner bar.

Turn around from the cooktop and you're at the sink—set in its own island—and ready to pass plated food over to an antique table that's used when meals are a bit more than grab-and-go affairs.

The three islands frame the kitchen in relation to the eating area and sitting room. They define the routes for traffic through and around the kitchen. Each island is deep enough so that both sides can be used for storage.

This kitchen was also ahead of its time in the way Peck arranged the storage space—in base cabinets rather than in wall cabinets. The three wide islands provide enough depth for drawers and cabinets on both sides. Only a single small wall has what would have been called typical wall cabinets back in the 90s. The other wall storage is a built-in, glass-fronted buffet.

Facing the breakfast room, the back island is the kitchen's cleanup center. The sink and dishwasher are well-placed to accept dirty dishes from both the breakfast room and the formal dining room, just beyond the doorway at the far right end of the room.

A casual sitting area and TV room, is open to the kitchen; family and guests are not isolated from the cook. The close-by wetbar lets guests help themselves without walking through the kitchen and interfering with the cook.

As in any kitchen without partition walls, structural requirements dictate what must be done. An addition provided the space for the new kitchen and the rooms around it, but left a roof span that had to be supported by ceiling beams and posts. Only one post was needed for that support, but Peck added dummies, creating symmetry and giving the kitchen a classic American Federal look.

Peck's open plan design meant that white islands at the front and back were related to the rooms they helped define. In the sitting room, the built-in bookshelves and other millwork had to flow naturally from the kitchen cabinets. To accomplish this, Peck hired a single cabinetmaker to design and fabricate everything.

▶ To Your Kitchen

From the Designer

USE THE SAME PERSON OR COMPANY to fabricate your cabinets if cabinetry extends from the kitchen to another room. **GOOD SOLUTIONS** often grow out of difficult problems: like the lattice above the wetbar used to hide a flue that couldn't be moved. **A BIG RANGE** requires a wall to back it up. If you want a completely open kitchen, a cooktop and ovens give you more design options.

Faced with a furnace flue that couldn't be moved, Peck built the wetbar, right, into the shallow counter space she had available and disguised the solid flue chase with lattice work. A glass front buffet cabinet, top right, holds both the family's everyday dishes and, on the upper shelves, Sally's collection of cream ware.

Welcome Warmth

End of the soccer season! This is where team and family members come to celebrate, eat, and relax. There's plenty of room for it: 1200 square feet of open space revolving around a new kitchen, large casual dining room, and a redecorated family room.

It wasn't always that way. The family room, 420 square feet of it, was there, but the old kitchen didn't serve it well and there was no place for a big table. The owners' decision to remodel allowed Moorestown, New Jersey, designer Diane Burgoyne the opportunity to devise a plan that gave the family a bigger, more efficient kitchen; space for the big, sit-down parties they like, and most important, a space plan that unified the family room with areas added by the remodeling. The three open rooms now work together as a single, multi-function living space.

Make it open. That's what the owners wanted. They told Burgoyne to give them enough space so that people could sit at an

Paint and upholstery colors are unifying elements shared by the kitchen and family room. Wall color and architectural detailing similar to the door style of the kitchen cabinets, along with a matching red fabric color used on the kitchen chairs and club chairs around the fireplace, help make these spaces appear as a single, open space.

island while other people sat at a table without feeling cramped. More than that, they insisted that when the chairs were pulled away there would still be 4 feet of clear passage so everyone could move about freely. For Burgoyne, this meant that furniture placement was just as important as appliance placement.

Openness is a function of space. With almost 800 square feet of newly added space under a 10-foot-high ceiling, there was plenty. Calling this a room of grand scale wouldn't be out of place. If anything, Burgoyne had to forget about tricks used by designers to make a small space seem large and figure out ways to scale the room back so it wouldn't overpower the people in it.

The kitchen layout is straightforward; the trench is arranged in an efficient galley. A large, twin-bowl sink in the island serves both prep and cleanup tasks. Behind it is the range. Away from the trench, a larger food preparation center begins to the right of the refrigerator and runs to the wetbar. The family's casual lifestyle and the meals that go with it favor cold food coming out of the 48-inch refrigerator. The long counter is used for both plating and serving this casual fare.

The well-equipped wetbar is where the family likes to use it: right behind the table, which can easily seat ten people, and close to the outdoor patio where casual American barbecue is a regular part of summer living.

Ceiling height contributes to the kitchen's openness. This height also allowed Burgoyne to design a decorative tray ceiling above the island. The molding around it breaks up what could have easily become a monotonous expanse of bland tone. Inside the tray, the red she chose matches the colorway of the fabrics in the family room, which helps to unify the two spaces.

Ideal for both large family gatherings and entertaining friends, the big island, right and opposite page, and the big table beyond it let people sit at both without feeling cramped.

The built-in wall unit, right, has a wide-screen TV that can be seen by people sitting at the island. Next to the TV is an aquarium.

A full-service wetbar with storage for both chilled and unchilled wines, below left, shows an ideal positioning of a work center along the kitchen perimeter. Though some distance from the rest of the kitchen, its location provides all that's needed where it will be used.

The big table helped Burgoyne deal with room scale because she could place eight oversized chairs around it, just as she put five large stools at the island.

Two other tricks helped scale back the room. The first was running a top course of wall cabinets up to the ceiling and topping them with crown molding. Since these cabinets are hard to reach, many of them are dummy fronts. Those without dummy fronts store seasonal items. Without these extra cabinets and molding, there would be an almost 2-foot gap between the wall cabinet tops and the ceiling. The second trick was choosing a very large fabric pattern for the window treatments—side panels that frame a window wall, which follows the curve of the barrel-vaulted ceiling.

This fabric repeats in the family room where it catches the eye and helps visually link the rooms. But more was needed to unify these rooms. The solution was combining new architectural detailing and strong color accents.

Burgoyne designed a fireplace mantel to cover up what had been bare brick. Above that, more molding to frame a painting and create a visual focal point. The molding's style relates to the door style on the kitchen cabinets; the finish is the same. The two large club chairs with ottomans, upholstered in red, balance the neutral wall tones and move the eye away from the high ceilings—exactly the same effect that the bar stools have at the island.

Totally Open

Barns. When you think of them, what comes to mind first is all that open space and all the things you can do with it. Judith Ann Paixao was thinking this way when she and her late husband bought this Connecticut barn, built in 1880, that had once been owned by George Balanchine.

It needed a major remodeling.

Paixao and her husband, an architect, had two goals. First, was to change the living area around by moving the public spaces—kitchen, living room, and dining room to the upper level. The bedrooms were on that level when they bought the barn. The second goal was building, as Paixao calls it, a house inside of a barn.

The barn's upper level had two haylofts, linked by a 10-foot bridge. It also had a 25-foot-high roof peak and all of the exposed timber framing that make barn architecture so visually appealing. It gave them the space for a totally open living area—an important

Barn red—what else would you expect in a barn—and natural wood are the primary colors here. Wrought iron door pulls and gate hinges on the cabinets add to the barn's nineteenth-century feel. So do the doors on the refrigerator. They are from an old icebox and were bought on the Internet. Judith Ann Paixao's carpenter adpated them to fit.

element when a living kitchen merges with the living rooms around it. This is where Paixao built her house. And that house has a distinct eighteenth-century feel. There are old pieces of furniture, some in classic American Federal, others in American Primitive. The interior barn architecture, while not diminished, is in the background, a frame for the decor, the antiques, and the oil paintings on one of the end walls. "You know this is a barn," says Paixao, "but it's the furnishing that strike you first."

The barn's upper-level layout determined the space planning. The kitchen and dining room are in one loft, the living room, across the bridge, in the other. In designing the kitchen, Paixao and her husband didn't want any appliances visible because they didn't want to call attention to the kitchen as something separate from the surrounding open spaces. They were helped here because there were no walls on which to hang cabinets.

At 150 square feet, their kitchen isn't large. They laid it out in a traditional U shape, with a small island that divided the kitchen from the dining room. It's just large enough for four stools so that people can sit across from Paixao when she cooks. And she does a lot of that—for lots of people—so she put a large commercial-style range in the island. Besides four burners, it has a

In a barn everything is open. In fact, barn layouts may be the historical prototype for today's open, living kitchen. In planning the appliance placement in this barn kitchen, Paixao put the range in the island, so that she could talk to guests in the dining rooms and also have a clear view of the fireplace in the living room.

griddle and a grill: more than enough to provide for the twelve to sixteen people who can fit comfortably around the dining room table.

An interesting twist in hiding appliances came about when Paixao considered the best way to hide the refrigerator. An eBay search came up with a set of early twentieth-century icebox doors offered for sale. She bought them and had her carpenter adapt and fit them onto her built-in refrigerator. You have to look twice at them before you realize there's a modern refrigerator behind them.

Barns are the last word in open spaces. Taking advantage of this, Paixao placed the island so she could look across the bridge to the fireplace in the living room. The island's central location also lets her talk with guests at the table or, more likely, when they have sat themselves down on the ladder leading to the barn's crow's nest.

But if barns give you lots of open space to play with, they don't give you a lot of options for kitchen storage. With no wall cabinets possible, the U-shape layout provided the maximum amount of base cabinet storage possible in a kitchen this size. Even so, more was needed. This took the form of a china cabinet, painted in barn red, the predominant color throughout the house. Paixao put the cabinet in the barn's silo, which in the final floorplan ended up next to the dining room. This puts dish, glassware, and linen storage close to the big 12-foot dining table. Also in the silo is a small desk.

The simple barn kitchen, left, is only 150 square feet. No walls meant no wall cabinets, which was fine with the owners, who wanted their kitchen to be indistinguishable from the surrounding rooms.

Family portraits hang on the dining room wall, opposite page. The table, with large chairs upholstered in red to match the barn's primary color, is large enough to seat sixteen people comfortably. The stairs in the background lead to the lower level.

Old bottles and jars, below left, are on display on a ledge where the roof meets the wall.

Ocean Breezes

Soft translucent blue, the color of the ocean on a clear day—this is the color of this kitchen every day. This is a summer house on the New Jersey shore—the beachfront if you don't know the Jersey slang for living on the ocean. When you live on the shore with the Atlantic as your neighbor, there is an irresistible urge to include the ocean in the way you live.

That's what happened here, brought to life in a collaboration between Michelle Slemmer, CKD, of Apple Kitchens and Diane Burgoyne of Diane Burgoyne Interiors—both Moorestown, New Jersey, firms. Besides ocean influences, the plan they came up with owes its inspiration to the curved stainless-steel railings that define all of the spaces in this house.

These curves motivated Slemmer to design an island shaped like a question mark, its convex end mating perfectly with the concave area across from it where the dining table sits. Other

A simple space plan, with the cleanup sink on the island and the prep sink in the corner between the refrigerator and the cooktop, is set up for cooking the lighter fare that's part of summertime living by the ocean. Ocean colors, translucent blues and greens, link the kitchen and casual living spaces with the long views of the sea visible out every window.

An **open plan** lets the **kitchen** and adjoining rooms enjoy great **views** of the **ocean**

The entertainment center, left, built into a wall unit of light wood, adds warmth to a color scheme inspired by the pale blues and greens of the ocean.

The space plan, based on the curved forms of the room railings, determined that convex and concave forms had to fit together visually like pieces of a puzzle—the inward sweep of the island suggesting a home for the round dining table. Above the island the monorail lighting repeats the island's question-mark form.

aspects of her plan are more straightforward: 230 square feet of space, a cleanup center in the island, the cooktop opposite it in a stand-and-spin arrangement, a prep sink in the corner. Outside of the trench a single refrigerator/freezer is at one end of an L-shaped counter, a built-in espresso machine at the other.

Putting the plan into practice was less straightforward. During construction, a big structural beam had to be added to support the clear-span ceiling. This required Slemmer to move the coffee station from the corner of the L to the end of the counter. The beam dropped too low to mount the espresso machine. A positive result from this was the addition of the corner prep sink and two windows to provide light for it.

The cabinets are maple that has been painted white. All of them are trimmed in stainless steel: box moldings for the tops of wall cabinets and toe kicks for the base cabinets. Six stainless posts support the boomerang-shaped glass breakfast bar that seems to float above the island.

With the kitchen planned, Burgoyne began to work out the color scheme and to design furniture to complement the open, curvilinear space. To create the shimmering effect of the ocean, she found one-inch-square translucent green tiles; she mounted these on the backsplashes. Playing off them are blue swaovoski crystals pendant lights dropping from a monorail above the island. Continuing the blue and green theme, she used a solid, pale green fabric for the bar stools and dining room chairs. In the living room a blue and green patterned upholstery fabric on the sectional sofa and chairs harmonizes with the kitchen colors.

▶ To Your Kitchen

KEEP YOUR COLOR PALETTE simple when coordinating indoor and outdoor colors. **USE WOOD AND FURNITURE** to add warmth to contemporary spaces and to make them appear less stark. **POSITION YOUR** work centers so you can take advantage of the great views through your windows.

This kitchen is a study in curved forms and stainless steel. The faucet, above left, with its bowling-pin–like base and bending spout, repeats the island's question-mark shape.

Stainless steel bar stools, above right, have curved back supports that sweep down into footrests. Their pale green upholstered seats play into the color scheme established by the backsplash tiles.

The Art Deco range hood, left, ruled out putting wall cabinets close to the cooktop. To make up for this there are two deep pot drawers under it. These are flanked by pull-out pantry units to store items normally kept up above.

The coffee station, **left, was fit into a modified pantry cabinet rotated 90 degrees—necessitated by window placement.**

Pendant lights, **above, dropping from a monorail, provide both task and ambient lighting. When on, the blue Swarovski crystals throw a cool, ocean-quality light across the room.**

Burgoyne saw the furniture as decorative detailing that would warm up the open, contemporary space. The Brazilian cherry floor that forms a backdrop to the shore colors—white, blue, and green—was conceived as a furniturelike element. She had to convince the owners that the darker floor created a better balance in the room than the lighter one they originally wanted, however.

The dining table, the bookcase built into the back of the sofa, and the entertainment unit add more contrast and balance established by the warm cherry floor. But the most interesting furniture elements are the dining chairs. They are classically styled Greek Revival side chairs, but rather than making them of wood, Burgoyne had them fabricated in stainless steel to fit in with the other stainless details in the space.

The People behind the Projects

INDEX